PATCHWORK
T-Shirt QUILTS

T0243990

Landauer Publishing

Patchwork T-Shirt Quilts

Landauer Publishing, www.landauerpub.com, is an imprint of
Fox Chapel Publishing Company, Inc.

© 2023 Amelia Johanson and Fox Chapel Publishing Company, Inc.,
903 Square Street, Mount Joy, PA 17552.

Project Team
Managing Editor: Gretchen Bacon
Editor: Christa Oestreich
Designer: Mary Ann Kahn
Proofreader & Indexer: Jean Bissell

ISBN 978-1-639810-23-9

Library of Congress Control Number: 2022951829

We are always looking for talented authors. To submit an idea, please send
a brief inquiry to acquisitions@foxchapelpublishing.com.

Note to Professional Copy Services:
The publisher grants you permission to make up to six copies of any quilt
patterns in this book for any customer who purchased this book and states
the copies are for personal use.

Printed in China
2 4 6 8 10 9 7 5 3 1

PATCHWORK T-Shirt QUILTS

The Fabric-Lovers Approach to Keepsakes and Preserving Memories

AMELIA JOHANSON

With contributors

Jane Haworth, Kristin La Flamme, Olesya Lebedenko, Sherilyn Mortensen, Jill Nelson, Stephanie Soebbing

CONTENTS

Introduction, 6

Helpful Tools and Notions, 8

Techniques To Know, 18

Working with T-Shirts, 19

Learning to Quilt, 30

66

48

42

114

70

84

Projects

Cross-Body College Bag, 42

Precut Dorm Pillow, 48

Concert Tee Wall Hanging, 54

Kid's Character T-Shirt Quilt, 60

Kid's Character Wall Hanging , 66

Rectangle-Block T-Shirt Quilt, 70

T-Shirt Tote for a Cause, 76

Two-Block T-Shirt Quilt, 84

Big Flight T-Shirt Quilt, 90

Improv Column T-Shirt Quilt, 94

Waterfall T-Shirt Quilt, 100

Modern Oblique T-Shirt Quilt, 104

Funfetti Caramel T-Shirt Quilt, 108

Onesie T-Shirt Quilt, 114

Glossary, 122

Index, 123

Photo Credits, 125

About the Author, 126

About the Contributors, 126

76

104

90

60

INTRODUCTION

Why Quilt Your T-Shirts?

Quilters throughout history have frugally made use of discarded clothing, feed sacks, and other fabrics not originally intended for patchwork, so it was inevitable they'd eventually set their sights on T-shirts. T-shirt quilting is a twentieth-century innovation—historians point to the 1980s, to be exact. This is likely because logo T-shirts became "the" symbol of children's extracurriculars, starting with a child's very first activity and continuing through high school graduation and beyond. Families everywhere, some of them quilters, were left with stacks of T-shirts, some barely worn, that represented various stages in their lives. Rather than toss them in the giveaway bag, the sentimental fabric-lovers cut them up into workable elements and sewed them back together into a sampler quilt top, creating a keepsake and popular graduation gift.

Today, there are no limits to what material or theme you want to try; whether it's concert tees, hobby shirts, superhero graphics, you name it, T-shirt quilters have it covered. Some even use outgrown baby clothes (and there is a design for that)! Over time, they've become more creative with their designs, moving beyond the traditional grid patterns, which simply join one shirt to another, into more complicated designs with sashing and cornerstones, fancy borders, and diagonal settings. These designs are great if you have a limited budget to contract a T-shirt quilting business or are especially skilled at oddly sized patchwork and piecing, but for a relative newcomer to sewing and quilting who wants to pour love into making an interesting T-shirt quilt on your own, it can be a little daunting. *Patchwork T-Shirt Quilts* simplifies the process, walking you through both T-shirt prep and simple patchwork, and lets you build your skills as you move from simple to more challenging projects.

I've combined T-shirts with beginner-friendly blocks and settings to give your quilts more design interest without being too difficult to make. Some of the designs are made with a set number of T-shirts with patchwork blocks cut to size, others provide options for a varying number of T-shirts of different dimensions, and still others patch T-shirts together with a more improv approach, so they are less reliant on the size of your logos. These projects use anywhere from a single T-shirt to 100 onesies (yes, 100 different baby knits) and any number in between. For those who aren't quite ready to tackle a whole quilt, I've also included a pillow design, two wall hangings, a tote, and a cross-body bag—perfect giftables. They can be made with a little nostalgia for high school days, tees from a chosen college, memories of a concert, love for your hobbies, a focus on awareness, or whatever theme you choose. Smaller projects are also a perfect way to use those smaller logos or extra tees that didn't fit into a quilt design.

Join me and a team of talented Landauer designers as I walk you through how to make a T-shirt project your loved ones will cherish for years to come.

Let's do this,

Amelia Johanson

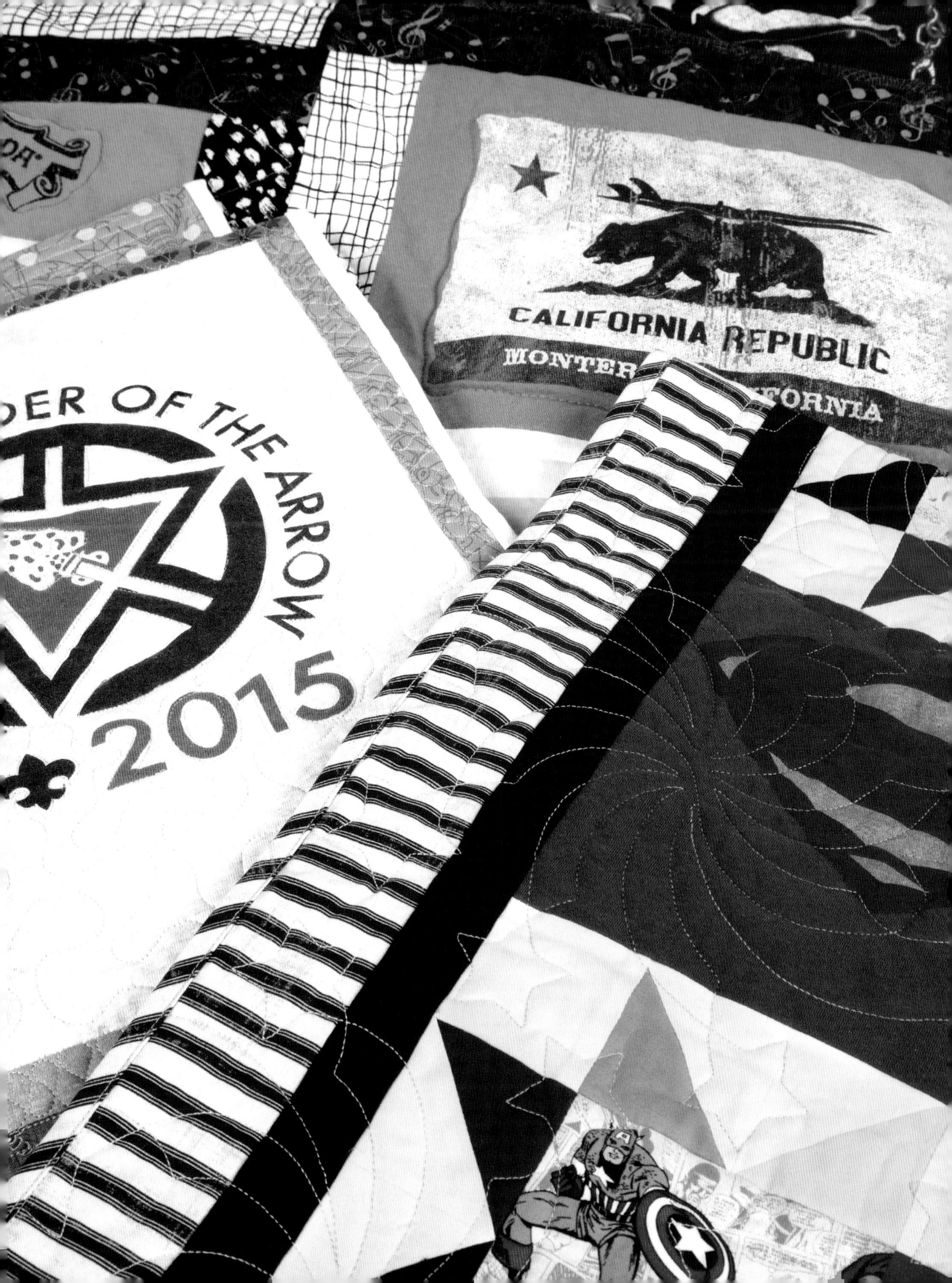
DER OF THE ARROW
2015
CALIFORNIA REPUBLIC

Helpful Tools and Notions

As with all quilting, you'll want a collection of tools and notions on hand to make the process easier. These items are what I found came in most handy when making my T-shirt projects.

Sewing Machine

The number one requirement for sewing and quilting is a sewing machine in good working order. Seasoned sewing enthusiasts will tell you to purchase the best machine you can afford. If you're trying to sew on a poor-quality machine, you'll end up frustrated with your craft. Beginners don't need a top-of-the-line computerized embroidery model, but they should invest in a quality brand-name machine with adequate room in the throat area. Some brands to consider include Baby Lock, Brother, Elna, Husqvarna Viking®, Janome, JUKI, and PFAFF®. Consider looking for models that are designed specifically for quilters, which will include a wider work area and specialty feet. It helps, if possible, if your machine has the capacity to move needle positions to the left or right to help in achieving accurate seam allowances, but it is certainly not a requirement.

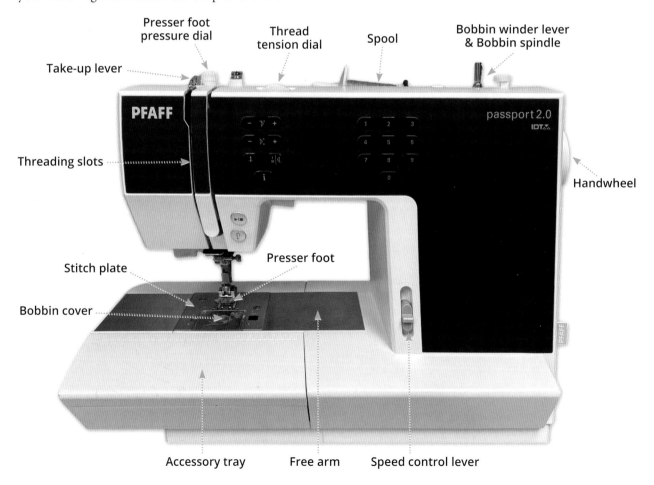

Presser foot pressure dial · Thread tension dial · Spool · Bobbin winder lever & Bobbin spindle · Take-up lever · Threading slots · Handwheel · Stitch plate · Presser foot · Bobbin cover · Accessory tray · Free arm · Speed control lever

Steam Iron

The number two essential investment is a quality steam iron. A steam iron aids in nice, flat pressing and in adhering fusible interfacing to your T-shirts, which is really important for stabilizing your knit fabrics before cutting them into blocks. Press your quilt units and blocks well and often; it's not a step you'll likely skip more than once. Always press in a lifting pressing motion; do not iron back and forth when quilting, as this can stretch your fabric.

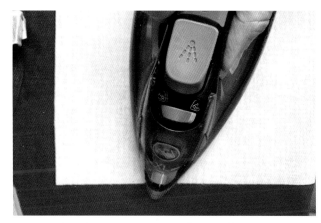

A steam iron is necessary to apply interfacing to T-shirts.

Machine Feet

The more you quilt, the more feet you seem to collect, but for a beginner making a T-shirt quilt project, it helps to have a standard **clear sewing machine foot** and **¼" (6mm) piecing foot**. Seams should be

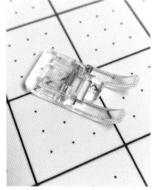

Certain machine feet can making machine sewing much easier, such as the ¼" (6mm) foot (left) and the clear foot (right).

Seam Allowances

A ¼" (6mm) seam in quilting is really called a "scant" ¼", not a true ¼", meaning it's just slightly smaller to make up for where the fabric folds back on itself. To test that you're achieving a scant ¼" (6mm) seam allowance, stitch two 2½" (6.4cm) squares together, press, and measure. Joined, the two squares should now measure exactly 4½" (11.4cm) wide. That needle position or guideline is what you want to use every time.

consistent and precise for units to stitch together nicely, and having a guide foot aids in achieving consistent seam allowances. Another foot that came in handy for these projects was a **zipper foot** used for applying piping and, of course, for applying zippers on top of the tote.

Needles

This tool is a tricky one for T-shirt quilts. Ordinarily when sewing on knits, a ballpoint needle is the way to go, as the blunt point slips between the fibers and won't cut through the knit, causing small holes. Certainly, you can use a ballpoint to stitch through quilting cotton. But since you're stabilizing your tees with 100% woven cotton interfacing and mostly stitching them into blocks, a universal needle will suffice. Size 90/14 or 80/12 works well for the projects in this book.

Do keep in mind that a fresh needle is important for each project, and if you're planning to do machine

Having the right needle for the right job will save you time and effort while you're machine sewing and quilting.

quilting or free motion, put in a new needle. If you're fortunate enough to have an embroidery sewing machine and plan to add embroidery to your design, use a machine embroidery needle. You'll see a touch of embroidery on the back of the Rectangle Block T-Shirt Quilt.

Pins

Select pins that are easy to pick up, have nice sharp points, and in a length that is adequate for quilting. It's important in quilting for pins to be heat resistant so they won't fuse onto your ironing surface or fabric when touched by an iron. If you intend to do your own finishing and will be securing a quilt sandwich (backing, batting, top) for machine quilting, you will want good-quality, curved (safety) pins made especially for this purpose.

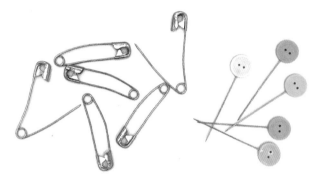

Curved pins (left) are handy for holding together the layers of a quilt sandwich as you machine quilt. Straight pins (right) are essential for piecing quilt blocks together.

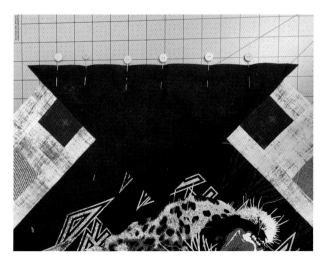

Quilt Rulers

Ideally, pick up a collection of **square quilt rulers** in various sizes: 4½", 6", 9½", 10½", and 12½" (11.4, 15.2, 24.1, 26.7, and 31.8cm). These clear, geometric-shaped rulers not only enable you to cut consistent blocks, but also because you can see through them, they aid in centering your T-shirt logos and determining how large a block each shirt can accommodate—not just the logo or artwork, but enough for unadorned fabric around the design and a ¼" (6mm) seam allowance to create your T-shirt blocks.

Straight, clear rulers provide an edge for guiding your rotary cutter and are a must for measuring and quilting. You should have a **seam gauge** on hand as well to check allowances. Although I didn't use any in this book, **triangle rulers** can also be helpful depending on your block designs; a 10½" (26.7cm) and 12½" (31.8cm) triangle are handy.

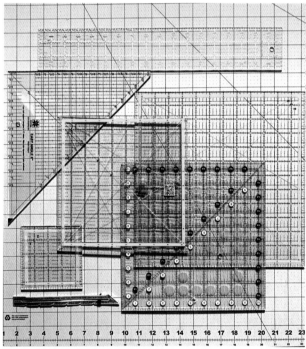

From top to bottom: Straight edge, 10½" (26.7cm) triangle ruler, 12½" (31.8cm) square ruler, 9½" (24.1cm) square ruler, 10½" (26.7cm) square ruler, 4½" (11.4cm) square ruler, seam gauge.

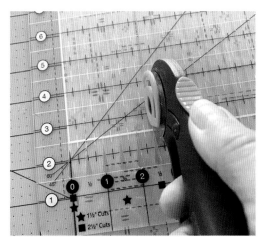

If you need to cut a lot of long strips of fabric, then you can't beat this simple but effective tool!

If you think quilting is something you'll be doing a lot, consider investing in a **Stripology ruler**. This specialty tool has ½" (1.3cm) slots across its surface, which accommodate a rotary cutter blade. Placed on top of yardage, you can quickly and easily cut and crosscut uniform strips and units for piecing.

Tip

A great trick for isolating the size square you need on a large, clear square ruler is to apply painter's tape to your determined block size. Now you can visually center your block. Cut two sides, rotate the ruler, and cut the other two sides just like you square up an HST.

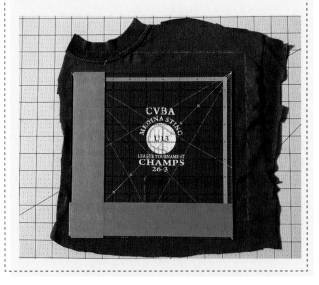

Tracing Paper or Wax Paper

While quilt rulers are your best option, as you can also pair them with a rotary cutter to cut your T-shirt blocks to size, they can be expensive, and if you're not a quilter, you may not have one. See-through tracing paper can be a good alternative for beginners.

1 **Measure and cut out the size block needed for the quilt.** Make sure all sides are exact and a seam allowance is included. Place the paper square over the prepared T-shirt and center the logo.

2 **Pin the template in place and trace around it using a straight edge and wash-away marking pen.** A ruler or straight edge placed in line with the template edge helps ensure straight lines if you're not a steady tracer.

3 **Cut the block.** After stabilizing the traced area, use a straight edge and rotary cutter or pair of sharp sewing scissors to cut on the traced lines.

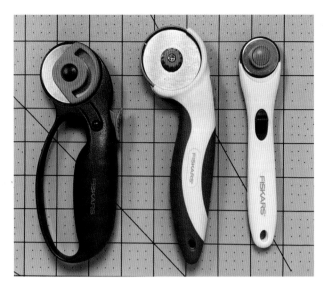

Rotary cutters are available in a variety of sizes and grips. The left and middle are great for cutting yardage while the right is perfect for small cuts.

Rotary Cutters

A rotary cutter isn't a requirement to make a T-shirt quilt, but it sure does make the cutting process a lot easier, and in most case, the cuts result in cleaner, more accurate edges. You'll always want to stabilize your knits (tees) before you cut (see page 22); even when using a rotary cutter, an unstabilized knit will stretch out of shape. Since all the designs in this book incorporate additional patchwork, it's definitely worth investing in a medium-size rotary cutter if you don't have one. They come in all styles and price ranges, but a $12–$25 cutter is suitable. Some have comfort grips, others claim ergonomic features, and there are lots of different brands.

The sharper the blade, the more success you'll have, so replace your blade once you notice it isn't cutting through cleanly. All rotary cutters have a safety-guard function; always engage that when not in use. If you're working with younger sewists, make sure you stress how to use a rotary cutter safely. To use a rotary cutter, you'll also need a resealable cutting mat and a straight edge; clear quilt rulers are ideal.

Cutting Mat

If you're using a rotary cutter, you need a cutting mat. Like cutters, they come in all sizes and brands. Select the largest one you can in your price range for block

cutting, and consider keeping a smaller mat next to your sewing machine for quick cuts. Self-healing cutting mats are best for quilting, as the material can absorb the blade of a rotary cutter better than a plastic or glass mat. Because of this, they generally last longer.

Sharp Sewing Scissors

Not every cut in quilting is best made with a rotary cutter. For any sewing or quilting project, you need good-quality **sewing scissors** on hand that you only use to cut fabric. **Pinking shears** are a better option for trimming seam allowances when you join binding strips. **Duckbill scissors** are nice for smaller areas, and they can be held flat against your cutting surface. They're ideal if you're including any appliqué in your projects, and I also used them to release the ribbing and sleeve seams on some of the smaller tees.

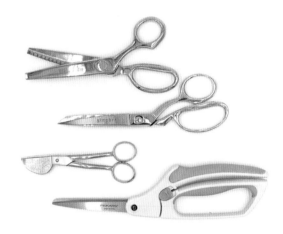

From top to bottom: Pinking shears, fabric shears, duckbill scissors, fabric scissors.

Marking Pens

The marks from **air-erase pens** are designed to disappear from fabric after a day or two. These are great when you're marking and stitching at the same time. You don't want to use them if you're marking your patterns and then coming back to a project later, because chances are your marks will be gone.

Wash-away marking pens stay until you remove them with a damp cloth, so keep in mind you will have to wet your project after completion in most cases to remove a residual mark. Clover Chaco Liners are ideal

Marks from wash-away marking pens (left) must be removed with a damp cloth while those from air-erase pens (right) will naturally vanish.

for T-shirt quilting and quilting in general. They come in a variety of colors. Silver or white are perfect for black T-shirts; pink, blue, or yellow work on white or other light-colored tees. The lines created are clean, due to a wheel application, and they maneuver beautifully. These are by far a favorite tool for the sewing room.

Fabric and Art Markers

With everyone drawing on their shoes and T-shirts these days, fabric markers have become part of everyone's sewing and craft room to add some personalization to any project. They're permanent and come in so many colors. You'll find them in several different brands and, of course, Sharpies work on fabric, too. Team with black-and-white comic prints or a simple white quilt cotton, and you (or your little one) can add artwork to customize a special quilt. Test your

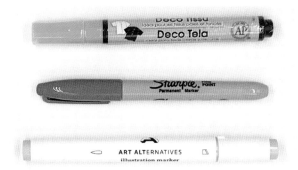

There are plenty of fabric markers out there, and all have their pros and cons. Experiment to see what you like best!

markers on the fabric you plan to use to see if you like the results or if bleeding is going to be an issue. I used a fabric marker to change the background color of a block in the Kid's Character T-Shirt Quilt.

Pressing Cloth

A pressing cloth is very important when you're making T-shirt quilts. The logos on most sports T-shirts, especially, will melt or become distorted with high heat. While you can press from the wrong side in most cases, there are instances where you'll want to press your quilt top from the front, so you'll need to place a pressing cloth over the design of

The discarded T-shirt back can be reused as a pressing cloth.

your T-shirts to be safe. You don't need anything fancy, just a large piece of white cotton sheeting or you can even use the plain back side of your cut T-shirts.

 Tip

Logos and other printed materials can sometimes transfer to your ironing board cover. If you think this could be an issue, it's not a bad idea to lay a piece of butcher or parchment paper on top of your board first, then place the shirt face down and press.

Seam Guide Ruler

This is a notion from Madam Sew that is particularly handy if your sewing machine doesn't have a ¼" (6mm) guide mark on the faceplate or you're not using a ¼" (6mm) foot (which is available with many machines). A two-piece tool, it enables you to sew accurate seam allowances from ⅛" (3mm) to 2" (5.1cm). Holes in the plastic alignment ruler accommodate a sewing machine needle. Once the needle is inserted into the chosen hole and the presser foot lowered, a magnetic sewing guide is positioned onto the face plate against the edge of the ruler. The alignment tool is then removed and you're able to guide your project against the magnet as you feed it through your machine for perfectly accurate and straight seamlines. It's especially helpful when stitching over batting and foam interfacing that have a thicker edge to guide along the magnet.

This handy tool breaks down into two parts: a clear plastic section to mark your seam (left), and a magnet that will stay in place while you sew (right).

Quilt Batting

To finish a quilt, the batting fits in between the quilt top and backing. This creates additional padding and warmth to the final product. Cotton is ideal and generally provides less loft than polyester batting. Wool batting is a lovely choice as well and is lighter in weight. For the projects in this book, I've listed the batting amounts by the yard in most cases, which is based on 90" (228.6cm) wide batting. The preference is yours.

Many of the quilts featured used Warm & Natural Needled Cotton, which is readily available.

This simple piece of fabric is an essential part of any quilt, serving as the center of the quilt sandwich.

Pillow Forms

Premade pillow forms are available in craft and sewing stores. The project in this book uses a 20" (50.8cm) form, but they come in various sizes. Make sure to consider the size of your form when you design your pillow cover.

Pillow forms come in all shapes and sizes; look at what is available, and maybe you will be inspired to create something for it!

Tip

Should your pillow cover design be too large for one size or too small for another, chose the smaller of the two and wrap your form in layers of batting before inserting your cover to create a nice fill.

Fabric Glue Stick

A water-soluble fabric glue stick is helpful for securing appliqués and keeping your binding in place for stitching. Some come in smaller marker tips for a more precise application, others look similar to what you send to school with your children. Use what suits you best.

Many beginner quilters prefer basting with fabric glue because it can hold layers in place more securely than pins and takes less time and effort than basting.

Printable Template Paper

If you're not particularly skilled in free motion quilting and feel more comfortable following a template, using a wash-away adhesive stabilizer is a great alternative for smaller projects. Sulky Stick 'n Stitch™ works like a dream. You can print line designs using your home computer, stick them to your project, stitch, then soak and remove the stabilizer. Check out the Kid's Character Wall Hanging for this technique.

Quilting isn't noticed as quickly as decorative blocks or bold prints, but sewing a unique pattern can add an original flair. Template paper helps you get creative!

Interfacing

It's critical to stabilize stretchy T-shirts before cutting into blocks for your projects, and attaching interfacing to your fabric is the way to do it. As with all sewing notions, there are all sorts of interfacing products available to you. While some interfacings will pucker under direct heat, 100% cotton interfacing does not, so you can press with a cotton setting against your interfacing (not your T-shirt), and it will keep your shirt blocks from stretching, add body, and provide permanent stability. Remember to use black on a dark fabric and white on a light fabric.

Pellon® SF101 Shape-Flex® is 100% woven cotton, lightweight, machine washable, dryer safe, fusible, and comes in white and black. On the bolt at 20" (50.8cm), it is generally wide enough for patchwork designs, but this product is also sold in 2 yard (1.8m) packages and online at 60" (1.5m) wide. Staple Sewing Aids also offers a lightweight 100% cotton fusible, which is 44" (1.1m) wide, although it's only available in white.

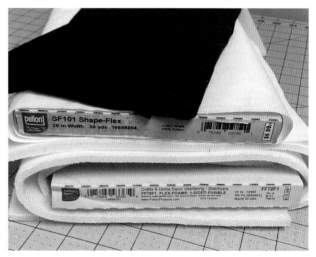

Stabilizing your T-shirts makes a huge difference in working with the material—save yourself a headache and always apply interfacing!

For adding dimension and body to the tote and cross-body bag, I used Pellon FF78F1 Flex-Foam™ 1-Sided Fusible web. This product has a spongy feel and also comes as a two-sided fusible. For straps and adding body to pocket pieces, a medium-weight fusible interfacing will do.

T-shirt block with interfacing applied.

Fabric

With traditional T-shirt quilting designs, which simply join rows of T-shirt blocks, fabric selections are relatively easy. Even if your design incorporates sashing (strips of fabric around the blocks and between the rows), it generally comes down to selecting one or two solids in school colors or going with a neutral that complements a variety of shirts. By incorporating patchwork into your design, you're opening a whole

A few prints from the Kasada collection by Crystal Manning for Moda. These are paired with coordinating prints that pull in all the varying pinks and turquoise from the T-shirts.

new world of prints. You want your patchwork blocks to enhance, not overpower, your T-shirt collection, and at the same time add interest to your design. Take your collection of T-shirts to the fabric store with you. Logos can have subtle color nuances that might take you in a whole different direction. Quilt fabric designers create collections for manufacturers, names including Moda, FreeSpirit, Robert Kaufman, Windham, Andover, and Benartex, to name a few. If you land on one print, chances are there are coordinate prints to go with it.

Selvage color dots can be a big help, too. When you purchase fabric by the yard, it will have a tightly woven edge down the sides of the lengthwise grain, which is part of the weaving process in production. It's often where you'll find the name of the print, the designer, and the producer's name or logo, but on prints, you'll also find a series of color dots. While selvages are generally cut off and discarded before using fabric for a project, if you save a section of color dots, you'll have the exact colors that are combined in that print, making it so much easier to coordinate with other fabrics that are not in that collection.

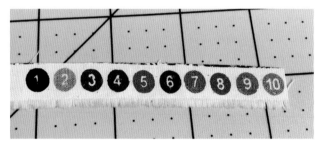

Utilizing these selvage dots can save you a lot of time and money wasted on buying the wrong fabric.

Precuts (fat quarters, Jelly Rolls, charm packs, etc.) can come in handy for patchwork and take the guesswork out of coordinating fabrics. For example, a Moda charm pack called Flirt created the perfect patchwork border around a red, black, and white college tee with a heart motif. Before going straight to the yardage, check out the selection of precuts. You never know if a precut collection might inspire your design direction.

Always keep in mind the theme of the quilt and who you are making it for. Novelty prints, like the licensed designs in the Kid's Character T-Shirt Quilt, work

Charm squares are not a resource you want to overlook! These match perfectly with the Precut Dorm Pillow design.

well for children's projects. If you're designing for an older child or adult, something more subtle might be in order. For example, rather than novelty horse prints for an equestrian theme, perhaps opt for Southwestern prints. The Two-Block T-Shirt Quilt features football tees, and while one of the red prints didn't feature actual footballs, the motif was football shaped for a nod to the theme. Grunge blender fabrics have become extremely popular in quilting; they blend well and come in a multitude of colors and subtle designs. They're also perfect for a more masculine feel. I used a black Moda Seeing Stars Grunge for the corners and backing of the Concert Tee Wall Hanging. Take some time to peruse fabric sites to see what's available for the design you have in mind. It's so rewarding when it all comes together.

From left to right: A novelty character print from JOANN Fabric and Crafts; Geometrics coordinate nicely with florals; White grunge-inspired print from Hobby Lobby; Moda Star Grunge in black; Geometric print with football-shaped motifs; Graphic strips are easy to cut and an attractive option for borders.

Techniques To Know

The projects in this book incorporate both traditional quilting methods as well as specialized knowledge for working with T-shirts. Even for the experienced quilter, it is beneficial to look through this section; when making a T-shirt quilt, you'll run into certain techniques that aren't typical in traditional patchwork. From determining a design based on the sizes of your T-shirt logos to adding quilt fabric to expand your blocks, you'll need a new set of sewing skills when incorporating T-shirts into your designs.

Design Inspiration

The quilts in the Projects section include complete materials lists, instructions, and quilt diagrams so you can use your T-shirts with the patterns in this book. But if you'd like to take a stab at designing your own, one place to start is with quilt books.

You'll find all sorts of inspiration, block ideas, and designs that can accommodate T-shirts with a little variation. For example, a traditional design (Christmas Confetti) by Lynette Jensen from her *Collection of Classic Quilts* book was the starting point for the Kid's Character T-Shirt Quilt. The 8" (20.3cm) blocks suited my collection of children's tees, but the on-point design was a bit problematic because it would mean cutting into the logos. Working with 10 T-shirts, and inspiration from Lynette's quilt, I created a crib-size design, alternating similar 8" (20.3cm) star blocks with 8" (20.3cm) T-shirt blocks, and finished the quilt top with a double border rather than the single on the original.

The key to reworking an existing quilt pattern into a patchwork T-shirt pattern is making sure your T-shirts can be cut in dimensions that will

 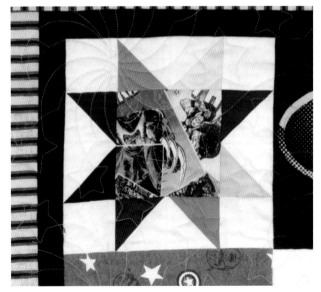

Christmas Confetti (left) was a great starting place for my Kid's Character T-Shirt Quilt (right).

work with the block size provided. If your logos need to be cut at least 12" (30.1cm) to accommodate the design logo, then you'll want to look for a quilt pattern that accommodates 12" (30.1cm) blocks. It doesn't necessarily mean your T-shirt blocks and your patchwork blocks have to be the exact same size. But you will want to make sure either the tops or side measurements of your T-shirt block match your patchwork block size. For example, in the Rectangle Block T-Shirt Quilt, the T-shirt blocks were cut wider than they were long (in a rectangle shape) with the side dimensions 10½" (26.7cm), the size of the unfinished patchwork blocks.

Just because they're called "blocks" doesn't mean they have to be square!

Working with T-Shirts

T-shirts are not quilting cotton; they stretch, the shirt or logos can be damaged by a hot iron, and they have necklines and sleeve seams that need to be considered when determining block sizes. If you're more used to working with cotton quilting fabrics, keep in mind that T-shirts take some extra prep. Once stabilized, they will sew beautifully into your patchwork design.

(Lower left) T-shirt knits will stretch and curl when not stabilized; (upper left) stabilized T-shirt block; (right) a selection of woven quilt cotton, which when pressed, need no stabilization and will hold their shape on grain.

Prewash

Some of the T-shirts used for this book were not previously worn. Instead, they were purchased, and thus not prewashed. If you decide to create a T-shirt project with a new T-shirt, always prewash it. Not all dyes are colorfast; in one case, when the iron leaked, the red dye of the T-shirt bled into the quilt cotton.

Because these pieces weren't prewashed, the red block on the right bled into the white blocks and the white print surrounding it.

Pressing

Many T-shirts have vinyl logos, which will melt or mar if touched by a hot iron. Always press from the back side, and if pressing from the front, top the area you're working on with a pressing cloth. Even when pressing the quilting cotton near the T-shirt block, it's easy to accidently touch the logo with a hot iron surface, so it's always better to be careful with your T-shirts. If a mistake happens, you can purchase additional quilt fabric, but rarely do you have a spare T-shirt of the same design.

Today, many high school and club T-shirts aren't traditional knit. They're a microfiber, nylon, or polyester blend. These can be used and should be prepped in the same manner, but the fabric can be melted or marred by a hot iron. Test on an area you won't be using to see what temperature your garment can handle, and always use a pressing cloth (woven cotton or T-shirt back) to be safe.

This vinyl logo very quickly and easily melted when my steam iron got too close.

A pressing cloth creates a safe barrier between the T-shirt logo and steam iron.

Cutting T-Shirts

Before you can stabilize and cut your blocks, you need to cut apart your chosen T-shirts; you're creating a flat piece of fabric. In most cases the T-shirt front (or back) will be large enough to accommodate your block, but always measure before cutting to make sure you'll end up with a fabric piece that is wide enough and long enough for your design.

If your T-shirt doesn't have a side seam, press your T-shirt flat to create a noticeable line in the fabric. This creates a cutting guideline up the sides and across the shoulders. Be careful not to touch the logo with your iron.

1 Cut the sides. Using sharp sewing scissors, cut your T-shirt up the side seams (or pressing guideline) to the sleeve edges. Repeat for the opposite side.

2 Cut from the sleeve edge to the neckline. Essentially, you're cutting away the back of the T-shirt so you're just working with the T-shirt front. (If your logo is on the back, the reverse is true; some T-shirts have logos on the front and back, so cut accordingly.) You can also rough cut your fabric to work with a smaller section. Just make sure you're leaving yourself enough fabric to cut your block.

Seam Allowances are Your Friends

Particularly when working with smaller or child-size T-shirts, the seam allowance previously created around the neckline or sleeve can give you that extra ¼" (6mm) you need to cut your block to size. It's easy to remove the neck ribbing or sleeves by snipping the serger threads, which are nearly always the way standard T-shirts are constructed. You don't want to just cut through these areas, as they could create lumps when you stitch the T-shirt block into your quilt.

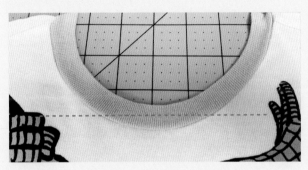

1 Measure your block size. After separating the T-shirt from the back, laying it out, and determining the parameters of the block you need, you may need to cut through the neck ribbing or sleeve seam. The dotted blue line shows where the block runs into the neckline.

2 On the back side of the serged seam, insert a sharp, pointed trimming scissor under the bottom half of the lower looper thread. I started with the neckline. By cutting through this part of the stitch, the rest of the serger thread will pull away. Just take care not to cut your shirt.

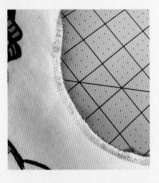

3 Remove the rest of the ribbing. You now have a flat ¼" (6mm) seam added to your cutting area.

 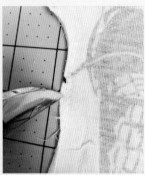

4 Repeat with the sleeves. The armholes, where the sleeves are attached, can also provide a little extra yardage. Like with the neckline, clip away the serger threads, being careful not to cut your shirt. Pull away the sleeve and press out the extra fabric.

5 Check that your T-shirt block will be large enough for your needs. Place your cut interfacing square over the prepared shirt. (You can just as easily check this with a square quilt ruler.) In this case, it works best to lay it at an angle. Notice how both the neckline and sleeve seam allowance are needed for the cut

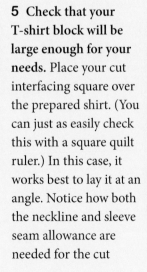 

Stabilizing T-Shirts

Now that you've cut apart your T-shirt, it's critical that you stabilize this fabric before cutting the blocks for your projects. When traditionally stitched, knits stretch and become misshapen without stabilizer, particularly when stitching knit to knit.

WATCH
HOW TO STABILIZE
THE SHIRT

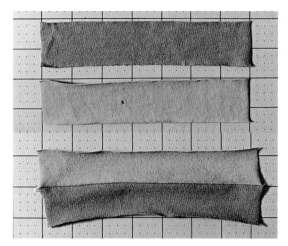

Two 7" (17.8cm) long strips (top) have been stabilized, straight stitched together, and pressed. They remain 7" wide and in the shape they were cut. However, two nonstabilized 7" strips (bottom), sewn in the same manner, clearly stretch out of shape and become lengthened, making them unsuitable for patchwork.

To stabilize a T-shirt, you to need to add interfacing to the wrong side. It's important that you use a 100% cotton fusible (see "Interfacing" on page 15). Make sure the logo on your T-shirts isn't too large to accommodate the block size you plan on using, and that you've also taken into consideration the seam allowance ¼" (6mm)

plus a minimum of ⅛"–¼" (3–6mm) unadorned frame outside the logo. This way you won't run the risk of catching the edges of your logos in your block seams. A good rule of thumb is to cut your T-shirt block so that you have at least ½" (1.3cm) unadorned fabric around all four sides of your logo. For example, if your project calls for 12" (30.5cm) finished blocks, you need to prepare 12½" (31.8cm) blocks.

To ensure that the measured T-shirt block area is completely stabilized edge to edge, you will want to cut your interfacing block at least 2" (5.1cm) larger (or 1" [2.5cm] larger all around) before adhering it to the back of your T-shirt. If you cut your interfacing square the exact block size you plan to cut from your T-shirt, you're leaving no room for error when you position on the back side.

NOTE: There are instances in which an all-over design, or large graphic, looks fine when stitched through or cut into. For the Big Flight T-Shirt Quilt, designer Kristin La Flamme purposefully cut through logos for a more improv effect. In these cases, you simply need to interface an area slightly larger than the block/piece you need to cut.

1 Determine what size T-shirt block your design requires. Cut your stabilizer square 2" (5.1cm) larger. In this example, the T-shirt blocks need to be 12 ½" (31.8cm), so cut a stabilizer block to 14 ½" (36.8cm).

2 Cut your T-shirt apart. Place the front on a flat surface and trace your block size, centering your logo in your square quilt ruler or template.

3 Place straight pins on all four sides. Insert one straight pin on each side, directly on your traced block line.

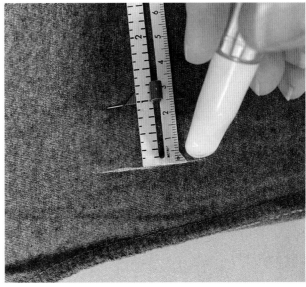

4 Turn over your pinned T-shirt. Using a fabric marking tool, mark 1" (2.5cm) outside where the pin is placed; repeat on all four sides. Remove pins.

5 Place your prepared T-shirt fabric logo-side down. Place the interfacing piece fusible-side down in line with the guidelines marked in step 4. With a steam setting, medium heat, press (do not iron) firmly for at least 10 seconds. Move the iron to another section and repeat, overlapping your placement and making sure you've fused all the interfacing. Turn, and with a pressing cloth, press from the front side of your T-shirt.

Joining T-Shirt Logos

Some smaller elements work better joined into a single block. Or you may just have more T-shirts to use than your quilt design calls for. In this case, you can combine T-shirts. Just like when cutting a standard block, you'll need to stabilize first, then join the individual elements together before cutting your block. How big you cut those rectangles is determined by 1) how many smaller logo sections you're using, and 2) how big your block needs to be. For this example, I'll be working with two T-shirt logos joined to cut a 12½" (31.8cm) block (12" [30.5cm] finished).

1 Separate your T-shirt fronts from their T-shirt backs and press. Lay one T-shirt flat. Fold the T-shirt you plan to join to it and position on top so that the logos are close enough together to fit in the block area. Remember to take into consideration your seam allowance.

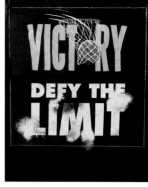

6 Place your fused T-shirt fabric on a self-healing mat. Check that your block guidelines are accurate, and retrace if necessary. Using a rotary cutter and straight edge, cut out your T-shirt block.

2 Position your quilt ruler on top of the T-shirts. Mark around all four edges with a chalk or wash-away marking pen. Remove your ruler and mark where the T-shirts overlap. This will be your stitching line.

3 **Extend the stitching line across the T-shirts.** For the bottom shirt, measure ¼" (6mm) above this line and draw a second line. For the top shirt, measure ¼" (6mm) below the first line and draw a second line. These second lines will be your cutting lines after you stabilize your T-shirts.

4 **Cut a piece of interfacing.** The two sections, which will be joined in this case, measure 12½" x 7" (31.8 x 17.8cm); cut two rectangles of interfacing slightly larger at 14½" x 8" (36.8 x 20.3cm). Stabilize each of your T-shirts behind the marked area with the interfacing rectangles. Refer to "Stabilizing T-Shirts" on page 22 if needed.

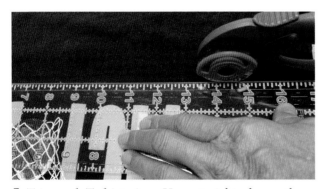

5 **Trim each T-shirt piece.** Use a straight edge on the cutting guideline marked in step 3. Make sure you do not cut on your stitching lines.

Joining Four Logos

Smaller logos can be joined in a four-square design and used in a larger block quilt. Each of these stabilized blocks started out 7½" (19.1cm). Joined, they create a 14½" (36.8cm) block.

6 With a pin, mark the centers of each prepared T-shirt piece on the lower cut edge of your top piece and the upper cut edge of your bottom piece. Right sides together, pin the T-shirt pieces together along the cut edges, aligning the center points.

8 Place your joined T-shirts on a cutting surface. Reposition your 12½" (31.8cm) quilt ruler and cut your block using a rotary cutter.

7 Stitch the pieces together with a ¼" (6mm) seam allowance. Press the seams open.

Joining Tees for an On-Point Block

For this shirt, the quilt ruler cuts into the neckline, but there isn't enough seam allowance available to complete the block.

Cutting a block on point (set at a 45-degree angle) out of T-shirts can pose a problem. Often the neckline breaks the cutting line, and if you lower the cutline, the logo isn't centered or extends outside the cutting line. One way to create on-point blocks for T-shirt quilts is to combine elements from two different T-shirts.

1 Lay down the T-shirt you're placing at the top of your on-point block. Fold over the top of your second tee. Place second tee on top to see how the logos will fit together.

2 Ensure the elements you need will fit in your block when joined. Position your cutting guide on top of your tees.

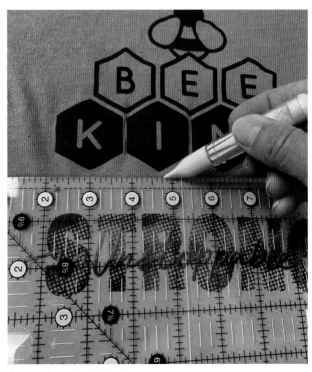

3 Mark on both T-shirts where you want the join (stitch line). Use a wash-away marking pen.

4 Mark your cutting lines. Measure ¼" (6mm) below the mark on the top T-shirt and draw another line across your tee. On your bottom T-shirt, measure ¼" (6mm) above the first mark and draw another line on your tee.

5 Rough cut your T-shirts. This will make the working area slightly smaller, but make sure to leave at least 1" (2.5cm) all around your determined cutting area. Stabilize with fusible 100% cotton interfacing.

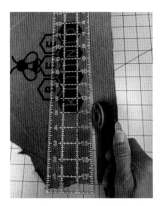
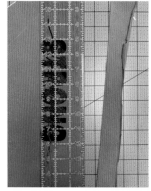

6 Cut both prepared sections. Use a straight edge and rotary cutter along the cutting lines drawn in step 4. Make sure you cut on the cutting line and not the stitching line.

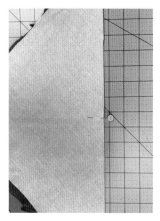
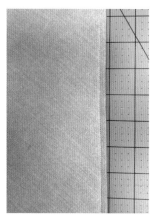

7 With a pin, mark the centers of both T-shirt sections on the bottom of the top T-shirt and the top of the bottom T-shirt. Place right sides together along the cut edges. Stitch with a ¼" (6mm) seam allowance.

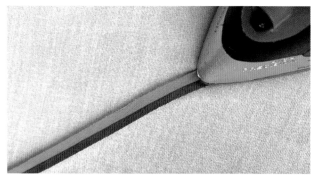

8 Press the seam allowance open. Place the joined T-shirt sections on a cutting surface.

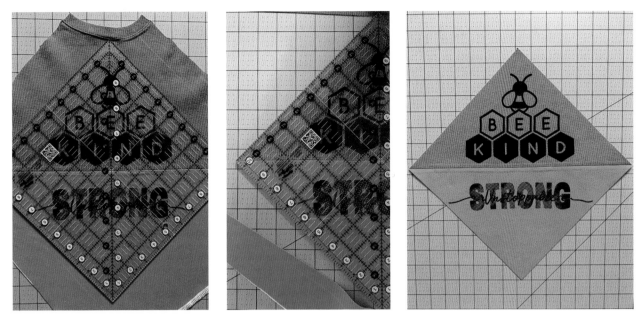

9 Position the cutting guide for your on-point block on top of your joined T-shirt sections, aligning the centers. Trim away the excess to complete your on-point block.

Extending with Fabric

Another way to extend the T-shirt area for an on-point block is to add fabric to the top and bottom of your prepared T-shirt panel strip. You could also add a strip of fabric between two T-shirt panels.

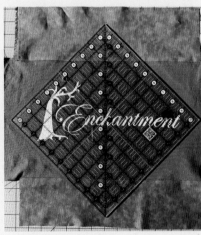

Learning to Quilt

Quilting is a craft that builds on your sewing skills. You'll find yourself continually doing certain tasks, such as nesting seams, making half-square triangles, binding, squaring blocks, and layering your front, back, and batting. You'll want to hone those skills so you won't need to revisit these basic instructions with each project. This section addresses the techniques you'll want to become second nature as you grow as a quilter.

Nesting a Seam

Nesting seams is encouraged when you're stitching joined pieces right sides together and the seams are aligning. On one unit, press the seam allowance to the right; on the other unit, press the seam allowance to the left, nesting the seam. Pin if you feel more comfortable and stitch.

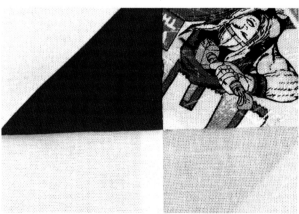

By pressing the seam allowances in opposite directions (top), they will create a smooth surface on your quilt block (bottom).

WATCH
HOW TO MAKE
THE BLOCK

HSTs and Chain Stitching Blocks

Piecing can go much quicker if you use a technique called chain stitching. Here, I use half-square triangles (HSTs) as an example. HSTs are a unit every quilter learns early on how to make, and they're arguably the most common quilting unit; they can be used alone but are typically combined into different quilt block designs.

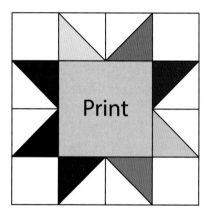

Print

The Kid's Character T-Shirt Quilt uses eight HSTs per block for 10 blocks. Rather than making 80 squares individually, chain stitching speeds up the process and saves you a lot of time!

This technique uses two squares and will yield two identical HSTs. Once sewn together, your original fabric squares will measure smaller than what they were originally cut due to seam allowances. If you need your HSTs to be 2½" (6.4cm), I suggest starting with two fabric squares that are at least ¾"–1" (2–2.5cm) larger, so 3¼"–3½" (8.3–9cm) square. Once sewn and pressed, your HSTs will be larger than 2½" (6.4cm), but you will square them to size using a quilt ruler. The larger you cut your original squares, the more waste you will trim off when squaring to size, so cutting fabric squares 1" (2.5cm) larger than what you need your HST to measure should be sufficient for most beginning quilters.

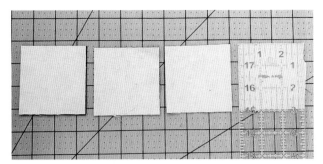

1 Cut the starting squares. Let's assume you need 40 identical 2" (5.1cm) HSTs for your design. Cut 20 squares in one fabric and 20 squares in another fabric, all 3" (7.6cm) square.

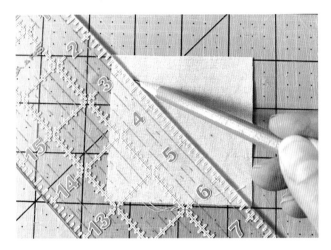

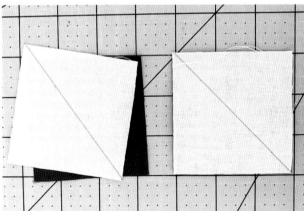

2 Draw a guideline diagonally from corner to corner, using a straight edge. Make sure it's on the **wrong** side of each lighter fabric square. A light pencil mark will generally suffice (if both fabrics are dark, use a Chaco liner). Pair each unmarked square with a marked square, right sides together, marked square facing up.

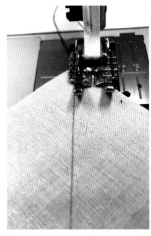

3 At your machine, make a few stitches on your first unit. Have the stitch line ¼" (6mm) to the right of the drawn guideline. Backstitch a few stitches then continue forward, stitching to the end of your block. Backstitch to secure your threads. Do not remove cut threads or remove the unit from the machine; instead, forward stitch so you're a few stitches off the fabric, then place another pair of squares under the presser foot, and repeat. Continue adding pairs until you stitch all the right sides.

NOTE: Depending on the number of units, you can choose to clip them apart for the remaining stitch line, or keep them joined. With too many units, they can tangle.

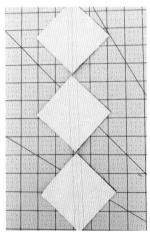

4 Once the right side of all units are stitched, repeat the process. Stitch down the remaining side.

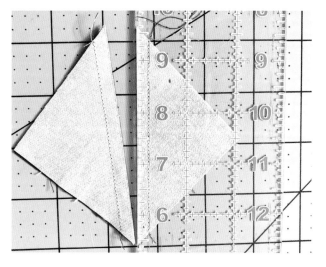

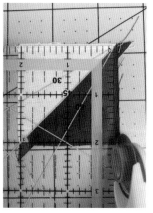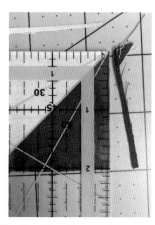

1 Place the stitched HST, aligning the diagonal center with the ruler. Make sure all the sides overlap your cut lines for your first cut. Using a rotary cutter, square off the sides extending beyond the ruler's edge and trim as shown.

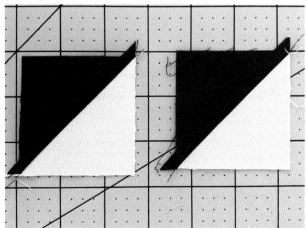

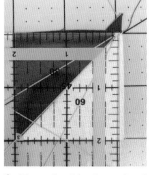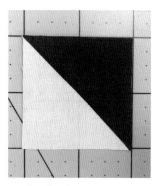

5 Cut each unit apart. Use a straight edge and rotary cutter to cut the unit in half along the original guideline to yield two units. Press each unit open. Your pattern will generally tell you whether to press your seams to the side or open, but a general rule of thumb is to press your seam allowance toward the darker of the two fabrics. You are now ready to square your units to size.

Squaring Up HSTs

Quilt rulers have diagonal markings for a number of reasons, but one very important use is to aid in squaring up half-square triangles (HSTs). Not only will some of your designs call for HSTs, your HSTs need to be uniform so they stitch together in a nice, neat patchwork pattern.

To ensure you end up with the size of HST you need (including seam allowances), it's easiest to create an HST that is slightly larger than what you need and cut it down to size.

2 Turn the block so the diagonal ruler line is again aligned with the diagonal seam on your unit. This time, make sure the edges squared in the previous step align with the desired block size labeled on the ruler; here, I'm cutting a 2" (5.1cm) HST. Cut off the excess as in step 1 and you have a perfect unit.

NOTE: All finished blocks should be squared to uniform cutting size before joining into a quilt top. Always remember you're cutting the blocks ½" (1.3cm) larger than what they will finish to allow for a ¼" (6mm) seam allowance on all four sides. For example, if your quilt pattern calls for a finished 8" (20.3cm) block, you will be constructing and squaring your blocks to 8½" (21.6cm) square.

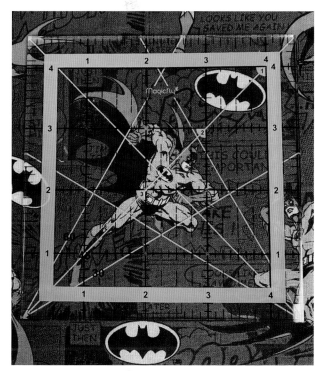

Play around with your print and clear quilt ruler; sometimes the perfect "frame" takes a little bit of maneuvering before you find it!

Fussy Cutting

When you "fussy cut" from a print fabric, you're selecting a specific section, often a flower or a character, so that it is emphasized or framed in your finished project. I used fussy cutting to select the elements featured in some of the center squares for the Kid's Character T-Shirt Quilt blocks. In essence, when using T-shirts in your quilting, you're fussy cutting all your T-shirt blocks to position your logo properly.

Template Quilting

If you are making a smaller project, would like a design element rather than just stitching in the ditch of your patchwork blocks, and aren't all that comfortable with free motion quilting, using printable, wash-away stabilizer is a fun and easy technique. Select an adhesive, wash-away stabilizer (like Sulky Stick 'n Stitch) that you can run through your printer. For the Kid's Character Wall Hanging, I found a star line art online, selected stars of varying sizes, printed them out on the stabilizer, and adhered them to the top of the quilt sandwich. Then it was simply a matter of straight stitching directly over the lines. Once you've completed your quilting, trim away the excess stabilizer and follow the directions for dissolving the rest by soaking it in warm water.

The template of the stars can be found on page 64, but there are free downloadable templates of all kinds of different designs online. Or you can draw out your own design.

1 Select your design. Scan the image into your computer if you've designed your own freehand or download and print out on regular paper to make sure the size is what you want for your project. Adjust if necessary.

2 Load a sheet of Stick 'n Stitch into your printer. Make sure you will be printing on the stabilizer side and not the backing side.

3 **Remove the backing and apply your template on top of your project.** In the photo, I cut apart the stars and placed them as desired.

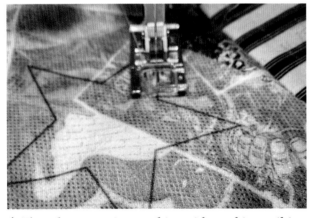

4 **Thread your sewing machine with machine quilting thread in the top and bobbin.** Straight stitch directly on the lines, stopping with needle down and pivoting if you need to change directions. Secure stitches where you start and stop with a few backstitches or lock stitch if you have that option on your machine. You can also leave long thread tails to pull through to the wrong side and tie off if you prefer.

5 **Make sure you're happy with the quilting once all the designs are complete.** Carefully trim away any excess Stick n' Stitch.

6 **Soak your project in warm water to remove any excess stabilizer.** Let dry.

Backing

Backing can be approached in a couple different ways. By far, the simplest is to purchase a single cut of backing or quilt fabric. For smaller projects, standard yardage (44" [1.1m]) may suffice as long as that width is at least 5" (12.7cm) larger all around than your quilt top. Yardage manufactured as quilt backing comes in widths from 104"–120" (2.6–3m), which is great if you're making one pretty large quilt or more than one quilt that works with the same fabric. What is more common is to piece panels of standard quilting yardage—two or three panels cut the same length and joined horizontally or vertically. It is recommended to use horizontal seams for quilts 60" (1.5m) and smaller, and vertical seams for larger quilts. What is critically important is to make sure your backing is 5"–6" (12.7–15.2cm) larger all around than your quilt top (same with your batting) as these will shift during the quilting process.

Incorporating T-Shirts on Quilt Backs

Your quilt back is a great place to incorporate a random T-shirt or two that might have special meaning but just doesn't quite suit your quilt top design. For example, for the back of the Rectangle-Block T-Shirt Quilt, I pieced the back by creating a center panel with two T-shirt rectangular blocks separated by a strip of the same width. If you have an embroidery sewing machine (or hand embroider), this is a perfect place to personalize your quilt to the person you're making it for. Once I joined the two T-shirts on top and bottom of the embroidered strip, I added equal-size blocks of fabric on top and bottom of the shirt block, ensuring the unit would be long enough for the required quilt back length. I measured this and added strips to this length on each side, again making sure the strips were wide enough to complete a quilt back that measured at least 5" (12.7cm) wider all around than the quilt top.

Another design idea: Many concert T-shirts have the band's tour schedule on the back. Rather than just discard them, consider piecing together your quilt backing to incorporate any tour blocks your shirts might have. Prepare and cut blocks from the back of the T-shirt just like the front.

By keeping in mind who this quilt is for, you can personalize the front and back with things they love!

Take inspiration from clever T-shirt designs! If it works for the back of a shirt, it might be fun for the back of your quilt!

Quilt Sandwich

To prepare for quilting and securing the layers, you need to create a "quilt sandwich." Place the quilt backing wrong side up, lay the quilt batting on top of the backing, and finally, the quilt top wrong side down on top of the batting. The batting and the backing should always be 5"–6" (12.7–15.2cm) larger all around than the quilt top, as these elements tend to draw up during the quilting process. Once quilted, you trim the excess batting and backing in line with the quilt top.

If quilting on a sewing machine or by hand, the layers need to be pinned sufficiently with quilt pins or basted to keep the layers from shifting during the quilting process. If you are taking your quilt to a long arm service (see page 36), you generally only need to provide the elements: finished top, batting, and backing.

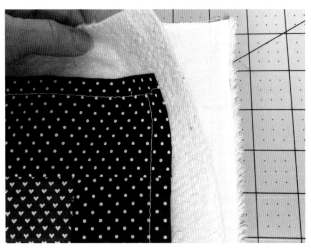

From left to right: Quilt top, batting, and quilt backing fabric. This is the same order that you should layer all your quilts.

Long Arm Quilting

If you're a first-time or new quilter making a bed-size quilt, you should probably take your top, batting, and backing to a long arm quilting service. This process of stitching patterns into your quilt sandwich requires special tools and skillsets. A search online will help you find a reputable long arm quilter in your area. Or check with your local quilt shop. Make sure you point out that your quilt top has T-shirts in it. Some home quilters prefer not to quilt them. Ask for a quote, which will be based on the dimensions of your quilt. Keep in mind that your backing and batting should be at least 5" (12.7cm) larger all around than your quilt top, as it can shift during the long-arming process.

Professional long arm quilters will also have a selection of designs. Take the time to look through the options they have available and select something that suits your quilt's theme. Often a long arm quilter will make suggestions if you're new to quilting or unsure. This goes for thread color as well. Spring greens or taupes tend to blend in nicely on just about any quilt top. A stark white or black can be a bit intense against fabrics that are not black or white, so often a creamy white or gray is the better option when you're dealing with a patchwork of colors.

Some machine dealers have long arm machines they rent by the hour, if you're so inclined; however, you will need some basic knowledge to get started, so I recommend looking into a long arm primer or taking a class first.

When you receive your quilt back from the long arm quilter, it will still have the backing and batting extended from the edges of the quilt top. You will need to trim that off before binding:

1 Lay the quilt out flat. Unless you have a very large cutting surface, it works best to place it on the floor and slide your cutting mat underneath the first edge.

2 Use a straight edge and a rotary cutter to trim away the excess batting and backing one section at a time. In the example shown, the clear ruler and the border are both 3" (7.6cm) wide, making it easy to end up with a uniform cut.

This off-white thread is a perfect accompaniment to the black, white, and red design.

Smaller projects can be finished on a home machine using free-motion techniques. Again, this is a skill that takes some practice, and there are lots of free-motion books and designs available. Very simple quilting on smaller quilts (up to lap size) can be done by following the seam lines (stitch-in-the ditch quilting). There is also the template quilting technique on page 33 for small projects. For quilting on a home machine, it's important to lay out and smooth your backing, batting, and top, and secure the layers together with quilting pins every 2"–3" (5.1–7.6cm) to keep them from shifting during the quilting process.

Binding

Once your quilt is quilted, whether you do it or take it to a quilting service, and you have trimmed away the excess batting and backing, the final step is to bind your quilt. This creates a finished edge around your quilt. Each quilting project lists the length of binding you need. Strips are cut from the width of fabric (WOF), which is generally 44" (1.1m) wide. For example, if you need 175" (4.4m) of binding, you will cut four strips (175" [4.4m] divided by 44" [1.1m] equals 3.97 strips) and join them together. Keep in mind that when you join your recommended 2¼" (5.7cm) wide strips with the method shown, you will lose approximately 3" (7.6cm) in length with each join, so make sure to cut enough strips; too long is always better than being too short.

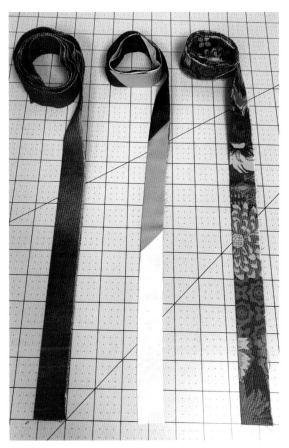

Binding can be a solid color, scrappy joined fabrics, or a print. Experiment to figure out what looks best with each design.

Calculating Binding

To determine the binding length for your quilt (if not provided), these are the calculations you'll need:

- Measure your quilt length and width, multiply by 2, add together, and add 10" (25.4cm).

- Since standard quilting cotton is 42"–45" (1.07–1.14m) wide, estimate your useable fabric width (minus the selvages) at 40" (1m).

- The most common binding strips are 2¼"–2½" (5.7–6.4cm) wide.

For example:

- Assuming your quilt is 36" x 60" (91 x 152cm), double 36" to 72" (183cm) and 60" to 120" (305cm). Add together: 72 + 120 = 192. Add 10 for a total of 202" (5.13m) of binding.

- Divide 202" (5.13m) by 40" (1m) to determine the number of strips needed. In this case, it's 5.05 (or 5.13) strips. Always round up, so you'll want to cut 6 strips.

- Multiply the number of strips (6) by the width of your strips (2½" [6.4cm]). This will yield how much fabric you need: 15" (38.4cm) of 40" (1m) wide fabric.

Joining Binding Ends

To join binding strips smoothly and avoid a lump along the edge of your quilt or project, it is best to join the strips with an angled seam rather than just placing right sides together and stitching a straight seam from edge to edge.

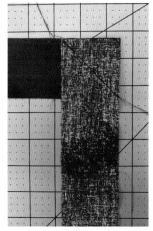

1 Join binding strips by overlapping the end of one strip perpendicular and right sides together with the end of a second strip. You should have a backward L shape. Draw a diagonal line from the upper outer corner of your top strip to the lower inner corner of your bottom strip. Pin if desired. Stitch a diagonal seam directly on top of your guideline.

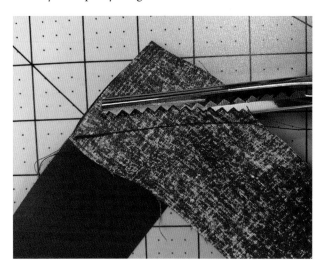

2 Trim the seam allowance to ¼" (6mm) with pinking shears.

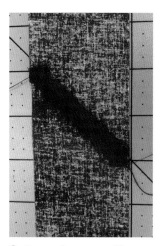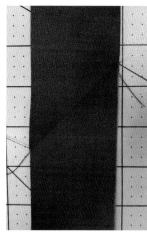

3 Press the seam allowance open.

Binding Quilt Edges

Projects in this book are finished with ¼" (6mm) binding. I recommend double-fold binding: cutting the strips 2¼" (5.7cm) wide, joining, and pressing in half lengthwise. If you attach your binding to the front of your quilt, I recommend folding over to the back and whipstitching by hand to secure to the backing. If you prefer to machine finish, stitch the binding first to the back side of your quilt, fold to the front, and machine edge stitch to secure. Both methods are used in this book.

Binding with a Whipstitch Finish

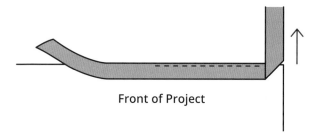

Front of Project

1 Fold the binding strip in half lengthwise, wrong sides together. With raw edges aligned, start stitching your binding to the quilt edge, beginning on one side and leaving at least 5" (12.7cm) of unstitched binding as a tail. As you approach the corner, stop stitching ¼" (6mm) before you reach the edge. Fix (or lock) your stitching. Fold the binding up at a 90-degree angle.

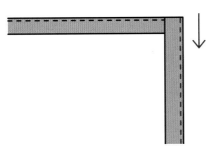

2 Fold the binding back down so that the raw edge of the binding is flush with the raw edge of the quilt and the top fold is aligned with the original side. Begin stitching where you left off on the previous side, making sure to fix your stitch line at the starting point. Continue around the quilt, stopping approximately 7"–8" (17.8–20.3cm) from your starting point.

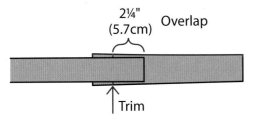

3 Place the tails smooth and flat along the quilt edge. The overlap will need to be the same amount as the width of your binding. For a 2¼" (5.7cm) binding, overlay 2¼" (5.7cm). Clip the excess ends of the tails perpendicular to the edge of the quilt.

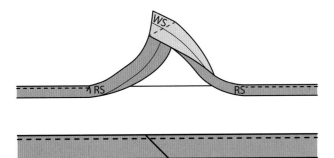

4 Place the ends right sides together at right angles. Stitch a diagonal line from corner to corner and trim off the corner, leaving a ¼" (6mm) seam allowance (top diagram). Now simply finger-press the binding into its original folded shape along the remaining raw edge of the quilt. Press, pin, and continue stitching to secure, fixing your stitch line as you start and stop (bottom diagram).

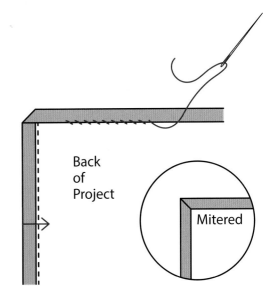

5 Press the binding away from the front edge and fold it over to the back of the quilt. Miter the binding at the corner and hand whipstitch into place with a single thread.

Binding with a Machine Edge Stitch Finish

Several of the projects in this book were bound in reverse; in other words, the double-fold binding was applied to the back side of the quilt first, wrapped around, and machine edge stitched through all layers to secure the binding to the front. To keep your binding in place for a machine finish, it helps to secure the binding to the quilt front with a fabric glue stick.

The binding on this quilt was sewn to the back side, folded around to the front, glue basted, then edge-stitched.

PROJECTS

Now, onto the fun part: Selecting the project that works with your cherished T-shirts. I've included a variety of different designs—including a cross-body bag, a tote, a pillow, wall-hangings, and of course, quilts in a variety of sizes—that call for anywhere from a single T-shirt to dozens. Use the patchwork blocks I suggest or pick a block you prefer with the same dimensions; there are endless options from which to choose. And if you want to sneak in an extra T-shirt logo, you can always combine two (or more) first, then cut your T-shirt block to size. One thing for sure, no two T-shirt projects are ever the same—even if you follow these instructions to the letter and use the exact same fabrics, your T-shirts will make your project unique!

TIP

Your phone is one of the handiest tools for finalizing your block layouts. Once all the units for your quilt are ready to be joined, lay them out on a flat surface, placed as you anticipate their positioning. Take a photo with your phone. Now look. You'll be amazed at what might jump out in a photo that you don't see with the naked eye.

Cross-Body College Bag

A cross-body bag detailed with logo tees is sure to win the heart of that high school graduate headed off to their chosen college. With pockets that easily fit a phone, tablet, cosmetics, and other sundries, it's an original gift you'll find yourself making again and again.

Finished Size: 12" x 10" x 2" (30.5 x 25.4 x 5.1cm)
¼" (6mm) seam allowance (unless otherwise noted)

Materials

- 2–3 T-shirts
  Unfinished block sizes:
  One 8" x 7¼" (20.3 x 18.4cm) for bag flap
  One 12½" x 2½" (31.8 x 6.4cm) for left side with logo
  One 12½" x 2½" (31.8 x 6.4cm) for right side without logo
  One 10½" x 2½" (26.7 x 6.4cm) for bottom without logo

  One 10" (25.4cm) x depth of logo for back pocket
- 15" (38.1cm) each of four different print fabrics: polka dot (A), plaid (B), stripe (C), and black/gray print (D)
- 1 yard (91cm) 100% cotton fusible interfacing
- ½ yard (45.7cm) fusible foam batting (I used Flex-Foam 1-Sided Fusible)
- 1 large sew-on snap

Cutting

From print A
  1 bag front strip, 2½" x 12½" (6.4 x 31.8cm)
  1 back pocket rectangle, 7½" x 10½" (19.1 x 26.7cm)
From print B
  2 bag front strips, 2½" x 12½" (6.4 x 31.8cm)
  1 back bag rectangle, 12½" x 10½" (31.8 x 26.7cm)
From print C
  2 bag front strips, 2½" x 12½" (6.4 x 31.8cm)
  2 lining rectangles, 12½" x 10½" (31.8 x 26.7cm)
  1 side/bottom lining strip, 2½" x 36" (6.4 x 91.4cm)
  1 strap strip, 2½" x 43"–45" (6.4 x 109–114cm)
From print D
  2 front flap border strips, 8" x 1½" (20.3 x 3.8cm)
  2 front flap border strips, 10¼" x 1½" (26 x 3.8cm)
  1 back pocket lining rectangle, 8½" x 10½" (21.6 x 26.7cm)

1 strap strip, 2½" x 43"–45" (6.4 x 109–114cm)
Optional: From any print
  1 inside pocket rectangle, 8" x 12" (20.3 x 30.5cm)
From fusible batting
  2 lining rectangles, 12½" x 10½" (31.8 x 26.7cm), trim ¼" (6mm) on all sides
  1 side/bottom lining strip, 2½" x 36" (6.4 x 91.4cm), trim ¼" (6mm) on all sides
From fusible stabilizer
  1 back pocket lining rectangle, 7½" x 10½" (19.1 x 26.7cm), trim ¼" (6mm) on all sides
  1 strap lining strip, 2½" x 43"–45" (6.4 x 109–114cm), trim ¼" (6mm) on all sides
  Optional: 1 inside pocket rectangle, 8" x 6" (20.3 x 15.2cm), trim ¼" (6mm) on all sides

Preparing the T-Shirts

1 Prepare your T-shirts with interfacing as described on page 22. Remember to use black interfacing if you're working with dark T-shirts.

1a For the front flap, position the logo in a 8" x 7¼" (20.3 x 18.4cm) rectangle so that you have at least ½" (1.3cm) seam allowance at the bottom and at least three times that (1½" [3.8cm]) above the logo. You want more space above the logo at the top of the flap as the top curves over the bag opening.

1b Cut a 12½" x 2½" (31.8 x 6.4cm) motif for the right-side piece, centering the lettering and making sure you have at least ½" (1.3cm) beyond the lettering. Cut a 12½" x 2½" (31.8 x 6.4cm) strip from the leftover T-shirt material for the opposite side and a 10½" x 2½" (26.7 x 6.4cm) piece for the bag bottom.

No wider than 10"

1c Cut around a second letter logo, leaving at least a scant ¼" (6mm) all around to embellish the back pocket.

Option: If you would prefer a T-shirt motif to serve as your entire back pocket, cut your back pocket piece from a prepared T-shirt to measure 10½" x 7½" (26.7 x 19.1cm).

2 Following manufacturer's instructions, apply fusible foam to the flap lining, front and back lining pieces, and side/bottom lining piece. If desired, apply fusible interfacing to your back pocket and inside pocket lining pieces.

Building the Bag

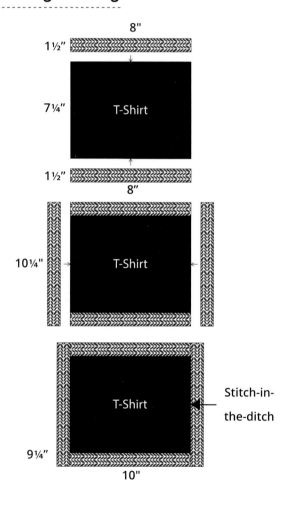

1 Stitch the 8" x 1½" (20.3 x 3.8cm) front flap border strips to the top and bottom of your T-shirt flap piece. Press seam allowances toward the strips. Stitch the 10¼" (26cm) strips to the sides and press the seam allowances toward the strips.

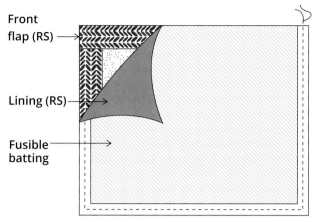

Front flap (RS)

Lining (RS)

Fusible batting

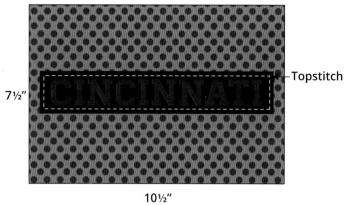

Topstitch

7½"

10½"

2 Place the right side of the pieced flap to the right side of the flap lining, and stitch around the sides and bottom. Trim the corners. Turn right side out and press. Baste across the top, close to the raw edges. Your flap should finish 9¼" x 10" (23.5 x 25.4cm). Set flap aside.

4 To make the back pocket, use fabric glue to adhere the prepared T-shirt motif across the center of your 7½" x 10½" (19.1 x 26.7cm) pocket piece. Because T-shirts knit won't ravel, especially when interfaced, simply topstitch just inside the raw edge with thread in a matching color.

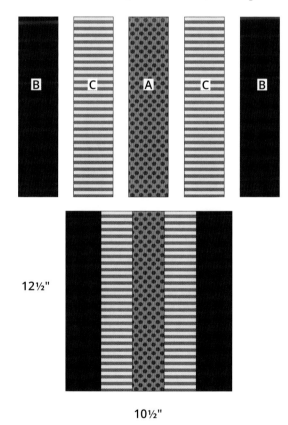

B   C   A   C   B

12½"

10½"

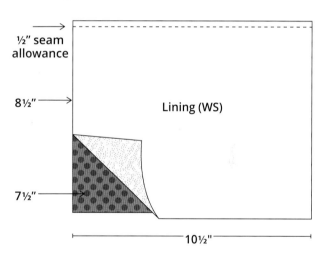

½" seam allowance

8½"

Lining (WS)

7½"

10½"

5 Right sides together, stitch the pocket lining piece to the pocket front across the top with a ½" (1.3cm) seam allowance. Your lining piece will be longer than your pocket front piece. Press seam with the allowance up against the lining side; this is to create a faux binding at the top.

3 Join your five 2½" x 12½" (6.4 x 31.8cm) strips in the following order: B, C, A, C, B. Press the seams open. Your joined piece should measure 10½" x 12½" (26.7 x 31.8cm).

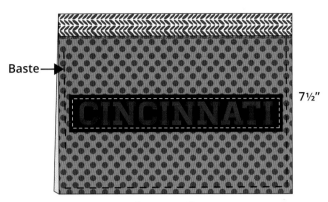

Baste

7½"

6 Fold the lining over the seam allowance, creating binding at the top. The bottom and sides should automatically align. Pin and baste the sides and bottom together.

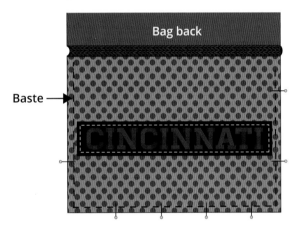

Bag back

Baste

7 Position the lining side of the pocket to the right side of the bag back, making the lower corners and sides even. Pin and baste down the sides and across the bottom.

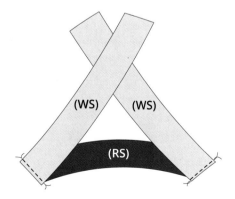

(WS)   (WS)

(RS)

8 Right sides together, join the T-shirt strips cut for the bag bottom and sides pieces. Make sure your right-side logo piece is facing so that it reads top to bottom. Press seams open.

Side/bottom (WS)

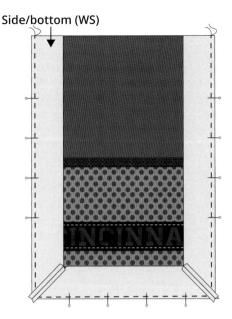

9 Align the tops of the side pieces with the top edge of the purse back pieces (right sides together) and pin. Now align the seamlines of the side/bottom pieces with the corners of the bag back and pin. Stitch around the purse back piece through all layers, joining the sides and bottom to the back piece. Repeat to add the bag front. Mark the center of the bottom piece and the center bottom of the bag front. Align and pin. Pin the bag front and the bottom at the corners and upper sides, and stitch as you did the bag back.

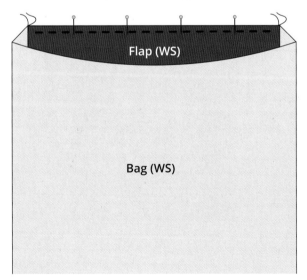

Flap (WS)

Bag (WS)

10 Align the top raw edge of the flap to the top raw edge of the bag back, right sides together. Pin and stitch.

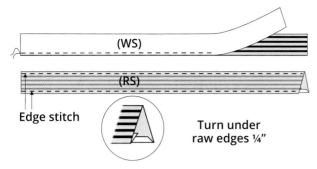

(WS)

(RS)

Edge stitch

Turn under raw edges ¼"

11 Create strap by placing prepared lining strip right sides together with strap strip. Stitch up on one long side. Turn right side out and press the seam open. Press the remaining long raw edges of the lining and strap ¼" (6mm) to the inside. Fold the strap wrong sides together and edge stitch. Now edge stitch down the previously stitched side. Fabric glue is helpful here to secure the seam allowance together for edge stitching.

12 Optional inside pocket:

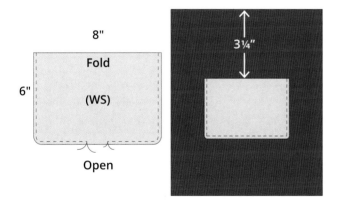

8"

Fold

(WS)

6"

3¼"

Open

12a Adhere fusible facing to the wrong side of one half of the 8" x 12" (20.3 x 30.5cm) pocket piece.

12b Fold in half wrong sides together (short end to short end). Stitch around the sides and bottom, leaving a 2" (5.1cm) opening for turning right side out. Clip corners. Turn right side out and press the seam allowance of the opening in line with the stitched edges. Secure with fabric glue.

12c Position pocket in the center of one bag lining piece (back). Pin and edge stitch around the sides and bottom to attach. Make sure to reinforce stitching at the top of the pocket to keep it from pulling away from the lining with use.

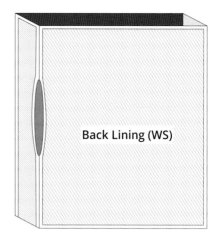

Back Lining (WS)

13 Create the bag lining by stitching the side/bottom lining strip piece to the front lining rectangle right sides together as you did for the bag. Trim off any excess side pieces even with the top. Attach the back lining rectangle in the same fashion; however, leave a 4" (10.2cm) opening unstitched on one side. You will need this opening to turn the bag right side out after stitching the lining and bag together.

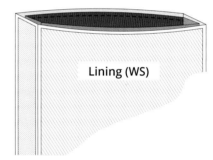

Lining (WS)

14 To finish the bag, turn bag right side out. Insert bag, right side out, into the bag lining. Right sides will be together and back of bag should be against the lining side with the pocket attached (if made). The right side of the bag flap should be flat against the bag back, as shown in step 10. Pin around the top, making sure the side seams on both sides are matched.

15 Stitch around the top. Stitch a second time to reinforce. Turn the bag right side out through the opening in the lining. Stitch the opening closed by machine or hand. Tuck the lining down into the bag and press.

16 Hand stitch a purse snap to the back of the flap and the front.

Precut Dorm Pillow

Occasionally, you serendipitously come across a precut bundle that's almost too good to be true, and that's the case with this T-shirt dorm pillow. I had an extra college T-shirt that just didn't quite suit the Cross-Body College Bag design—a little too large, a bit of a busy graphic—and set it aside . . . until I spotted Moda's Flirt Charm Pack. It couldn't have been more perfect to coordinate with my rogue shirt, and this project is truly simple to create.

Finished Size: 19½" x 19½" (49.5 x 49.5cm)

Materials

- 1 graphic T-shirt
  Unfinished block size: One 12½" x 12½" (31.8 x 31.8cm)
- 1 mini-charm pack that coordinates with T-shirt
- ¾ yards (69cm) solid-color fabric or subtle-print fabric for sashing and pillow back
- 25" x 25" (63.5 x 63.5cm) batting
- 25" x 25" (63.5 x 63.5cm) lining fabric
- ½ yard (45.7cm) 100% cotton fusible interfacing
- Optional: 2¼ yards (2m) prepackaged piping
- 20" (50.8cm) pillow form

Cutting

From charm pack (or assorted prints):
   30 assorted squares, 2½" (6.4cm)
From solid or print fabric
   2 sashing strips, 2¾" x 16½" (7 x 41.9cm)
   2 sashing strips, 2¾" x 21" (7 x 53.3cm)
From solid or print fabric
   2 pillow back rectangles, 21" x 14" (53.3 x 35.6cm)

Instructions

1 Prepare your T-shirt with interfacing as described on page 22. Cut your T-shirt apart so you are working with a single layer. Using a quilt ruler or the tracing paper method, interface and cut out your design so that it finishes 12½" (31.8cm) square and the design is centered.

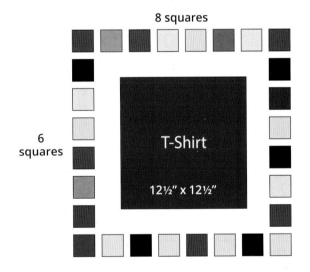

8 squares

6 squares

T-Shirt

12½" x 12½"

2 Place your square on a flat surface and arrange your charm squares. You will need six squares on each side and eight squares across the top and bottom.

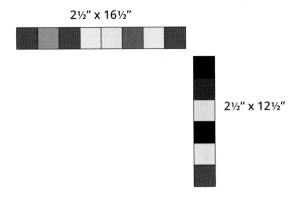

2½" x 16½"

2½" x 12½"

3 Working side by side, join the squares together using a ¼" (6mm) seam allowance. Your six squares will join to finish 12½" (31.8cm). Your eight squares will join to finish 16½" (41.9cm). Press the seam allowances between your squares open.

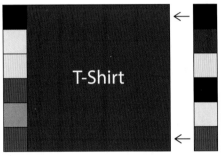

4 Join the 12½" (31.8cm) side rows to the sides of your quilt T-shirt center using a ¼" (6mm) seam allowance. Press the seam allowances away from the T-shirt center.

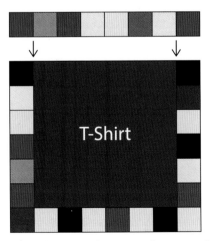

5 Join the 16½" (31.8cm) rows to the top and bottom using a ¼" (6mm) seam allowance. Press the seam allowances away from the T-shirt center.

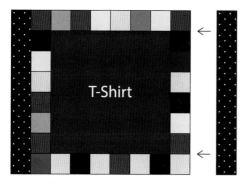

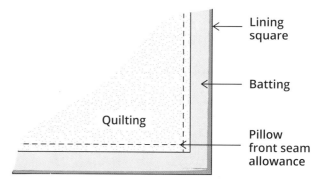

Lining square

Batting

Quilting

Pillow front seam allowance

6 Join the 2¾" x 16½" (7 x 41.9cm) sashing strips to the sides of your pillow top center. Press the seam allowances toward the sashing. Trim sashing strips even with the pillow top and bottom edges.

9 Layer the pillow top with 25" (63.5cm) squares of batting and lining to make a quilt sandwich. Pin to secure. Quilt as desired. Only take one or two stitches outside the seam allowance guideline.

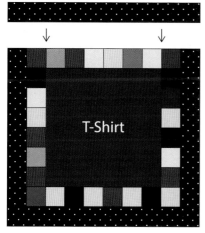

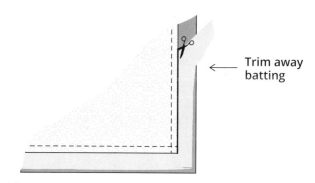

Trim away batting

7 Join the 2¾" x 21" (7 x 53.3cm) sashing strips to the top and bottom of your pillow center. Press the seam allowances toward the sashing. Trim sashing strips even with the pillow side edges.

10 Once quilting is complete, trim only the batting outside the seam allowance line, being careful not to cut the pillow front or lining.

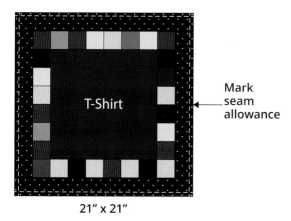

Mark seam allowance

21" x 21"

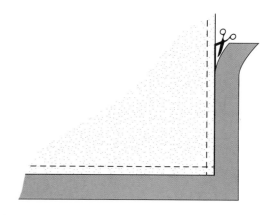

11 Trim the lining even with your pillow top.

8 Optional: With a wash-away marker, mark the ½" (1.3cm) seam allowance line on the front side of the pillow front on all four sides.

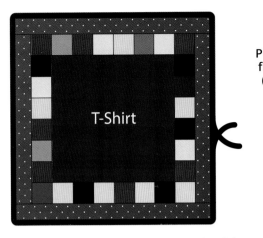

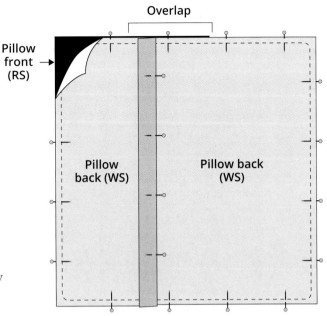

12 Optional: Position piping on the right side of the pillow so the stitching line of the piping is directly over the seam allowance stitching. Using a piping foot, apply the piping all the way around the pillow.

14 Working from the wrong sides, overlap the backs on the finished edges so together they measure 21" (53.3cm) square. Pin down the center through both layers. Place on top of the right side of the pillow front, right sides of pillow to right sides of back. Pin around all four sides and stitch with a ½" (1.3cm) seam allowance.

> ## Tip
>
> Use a zipper foot and a left needle position to apply your piping. It lets your needle pierce directly on the stitch line of your prepared piping for a nice, neat application.

15 Remove the pins, clip across the corners close to the stitching, and turn the pillow cover right sides out through the back opening. If piped, tug gently on the piping; if not piped, push out the corners with a blunt but pointed object. Remove pins on overlap. Insert a 20" (50.1cm) pillow form.

13 Fold ¼" (6mm) back on one 21" (53.3cm) side of a pillow back rectangle. Press. Fold under another 1" (2.5cm) and press. Edge stitch along the fold to secure and finish. Repeat for the second rectangle on one 21" (53.3cm) side.

Concert Tee Wall Hanging

Long arm quilted by The Little Red Quilt House, Medina County, Ohio

Featuring four of your favorite concert tees, this wall hanging has the added design element of contrast corners that add the sensibility of frame corners commonly used to protect photo memories in scrapbooks. The binding is also done in two colors, black around the corners and white along the sides, so it takes a bit of careful placement when joining the binding strips. The patchwork block used here is called the Bright Hopes block.

Finished Size: 44½" x 44½" (1.1 x 1.1m)
¼" seam allowance throughout

Materials

- 4 T-shirts
  Unfinished block size: Four 16½" x 16½" (41.9 x 41.9cm)
- One 2½" (6.4cm) strip each of red, blue, yellow, and orange prints for block centers
- ½ yard (45.7cm) black-and-white graphic print for blocks, corners, sashing, and binding*
- ⅓ yard (30.5cm) black star grunge print for corners and binding*
  *Cut binding in 8 separate 2¼" (5.7cm) strips, 4 black-and-white and 4 black
- 4" x 44" (10.2 x 111.8cm) black quilt binding for hanging sleeve
- 54" x 54" (1.4 x 1.4m) quilt backing fabric
- 54" x 54" (1.4 x 1.4m) batting

Cutting

From each blue, yellow, and red print
  8 block squares, 2½" (6.4cm)

From orange print
  5 block squares, 2½" (6.4cm)

From white and black print
  116 block strips, 3½" x 1½" (8.9 x 3.8cm)
  4 corner squares, 5½" (14cm), cut corner to corner to create 8 triangles
  4 sashing strips, 16½" x 4½" (41.9 x 11.4cm)
  4 binding strips, 2¼" x 36" (5.7 x 91.4cm)

From black grunge print
  2 corner squares, 12½" (31.8cm), cut corner to corner to create 4 triangles
  4 binding strips, 2¼" x 18" (5.7 x 45.7cm)

Making the Blocks

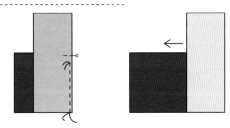

1 Place one white 3½" x 1½" (9 x 3.8cm) strip on top of a color 2½" (6.4cm) square right sides together so that the lower-right corners and right sides align as shown. **NOTE:** Every Bright Hope unit must start out positioned the same way so the seams align when you arrange them for the quilt top. Pin if desired, and stitch from the center of the right side to the bottom of the unit. You will only be stitching a partial seam in this step. Press open with seam toward the center square.

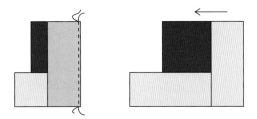

2 With the partially stitched strip positioned across the bottom, place a second strip. Keep right sides together to the right side of the unit, corners and sides aligned as shown. Stitch from top to bottom. This will be a complete seam. Press open with the seam toward the center square.

3 Add the third strip as you did in step 2, working around the center square and pressing open with the seam allowance toward the center.

 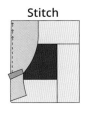 

Stitch

4½" x 4½" Make 8

4 To complete the block, align the partially stitched strip from step 1, right sides together, with the center square and the top edge of strip 3. Insert your needle where the first stitching line stops in the center.

Backstitch over the stitch line to start, then stitch forward to secure the first strip. Open and press the seam allowance toward the center. Check that your block is 4½" (11.4cm) square. Square up with a ruler if not, making sure the side strips finish 1¼" (3.2cm) wide and the center square measures 2" (5.1cm).

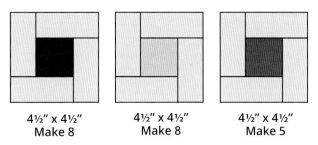

4½" x 4½"
Make 8

4½" x 4½"
Make 8

4½" x 4½"
Make 5

5 Repeat steps 1–4 to make eight red, eight yellow, eight blue, and five orange Bright Hopes blocks.

Building the Quilt

1 Prepare and cut your T-shirts to create four 16½" (41.9cm) square T-shirt blocks, centering the motifs. Refer to "Stabilizing T-Shirts" on page 22 and "Cutting T-Shirts" on page 20. **NOTE:** Use black stabilizer for darker tees, white for lighter tees.

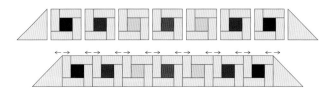

2 Create four identical quilt borders with the following pieces (as shown): white triangle, red, blue, yellow, orange, yellow, blue, red, and white triangle. Since you made each block in the same order, the seams of your blocks should align and nest for construction. Your triangles will be flat on the bottom and side, with the angled edge facing upward as shown. Join the units in each row. Press seams open.

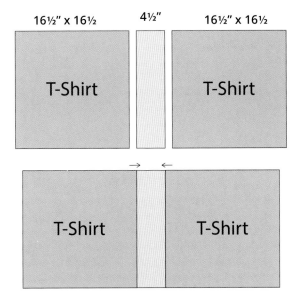

16½" x 16½" 4½" 16½" x 16½"

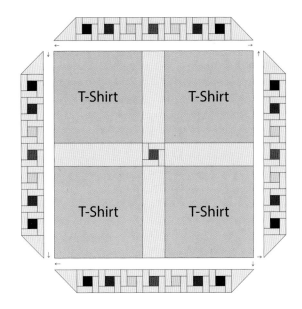

3 Join two T-shirt blocks with a sashing strip in the center. Repeat for the second two T-shirt blocks. Press the seams away from the T-shirt blocks.

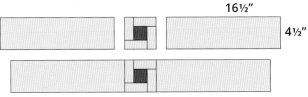

16½"

4½"

4 Join your final orange Bright Hopes block to the remaining two sashing strips as shown. Press the seam allowances toward center block.

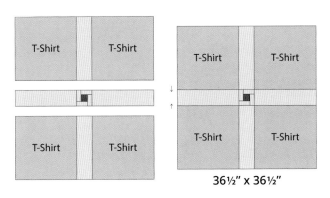

36½" x 36½"

5 Right sides together, join the top T-shirt row to the center sashing row, nesting the seams. Repeat with the bottom T-shirt row.

6 Stitch the block borders created in step 2 to the top and bottom of the quilt center. Repeat with the side block borders. Press the seam allowances away from center.

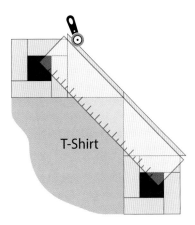

7 Using a straight edge and rotary cutter, true up the angle across each of the four corners in preparation for adding the final black corner units. Position the straight edge so that you will have a ¼" (6mm) seam allowance at the side edges.

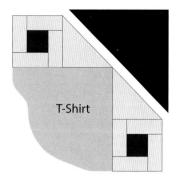

8 Right sides together, center and join a black triangle unit to each corner. Your black corners will overhang the edges and be slightly larger than needed. This will allow you to true up 90-degree corners on your quilt after long-arming or quilting by domestic machine, which can draw in the edges slightly.

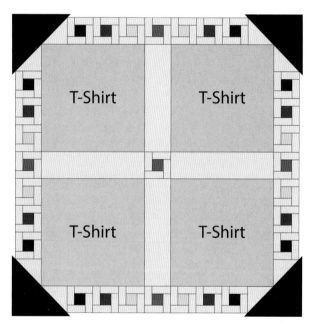

9 Layer and quilt as desired.

Binding

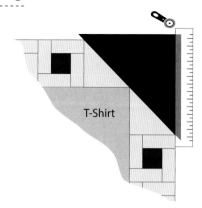

1 Trim away any batting and backing, using a straight edge to true up each corner in line with the sides of the quilt.

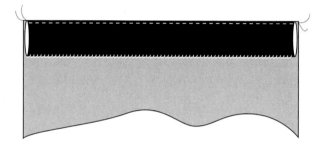

2 Prepare and add a hanging sleeve to the top edge of your quilt using your black 4" x 44" (10.2 x 111.8cm) strip. Fold and press the short ends to the wrong side ¼" (6mm), then topstitch to secure. Fold the strip lengthwise, wrong sides together, and press. Center and pin with long raw edges to the top edge of your wall hanging on the wrong side; pin and baste with a ¼" (6mm) seam allowance. Whipstitch the lower edge to your quilt back.

3 Join one black-and-white strip to one black grunge strip as you would typically join binding (see page 38). With this technique, the seam line automatically joins on the diagonal. Press the strip in half lengthwise.

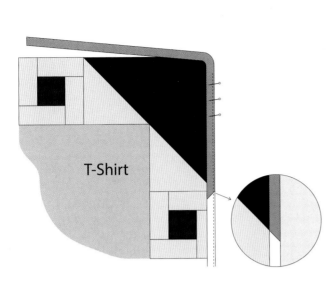

4 On the front of your quilt, you will want to start stitching your binding, pinning the join of your binding strip to the join of one of the corner units. Since you will be stitching right sides together, you'll want to check the alignment carefully before pinning. The angle of the join will face the wrong direction when the binding is placed right side down on the quilt edge. Once it's stitched and flipped, it will angle the right direction. Make sure the unstitched end of your black binding strip will be long enough to go around the corner and create an angled join on the opposite side of your triangle.

5 Stitch your binding strip to one side, stopping approximately 6" (15.2cm) before you come to the next black corner unit. Place the white binding strip against the quilt edge and mark where you'll need the next black strip to begin. Keep in mind the ¼" (6mm) seam allowance and that this join will need to be angled in the opposite direction from the first. Join the next black strip to your white strip where marked. Press in half, check placement, and continue stitching the binding on the quilt.

6 Repeat the process of joining binding strips prior to approaching the beginning or end of a corner unit and making sure your joins are angled in the right direction. When you approach the corner unit where you started, stop stitching the white binding strip. Stitch the unattached end of the first black strip around the corner. Stop stitching about halfway to the end of the corner unit and join the white strip to the black strip as you did for the previous corners. Miter the black binding in the corners and finish your binding like you typically would.

7 Press and fold your binding to the wrong side and hand stitch to the back side of your quilt to secure.

Kid's Character T-Shirt Quilt

Long arm quilted by The Little Red Quilt House, Medina County, Ohio

What little one doesn't love superheroes? Their drawers are filled with character tees and pj's because superheroes are colorful, fearless, and part of countless childhood memories. Here, T-shirt blocks are paired with bright patchwork star blocks, pieced from licensed prints, bold solids, and a bit of fussy cutting. A star and swirls quilting design makes the perfect pairing. Licensed characters of all kinds can be found in tees and fabrics, and this design is perfect for whichever one is your child's favorite, from Star Wars to Hello Kitty and Disney Princesses to Pokémon.

Finished Size: 39" x 47" (99.1 x 119.4cm)
¼" (6mm) seam allowance (unless otherwise noted)

Materials

- 10 T-shirts with superhero logos
  Unfinished block size:
  Ten 8½" x 8½" (21.6 x 21.6cm)
  Ten 5" x 5" (12.7 x 12.7cm) assorted character prints
- One 4" (10.2cm) strip each of black, brown, green, blue, red, light blue, orange, and yellow solid-color quilt cotton
- ½ yard (45.7cm) cream quilt cotton
- ¼ yard (22.9cm) black quilt cotton for inner border
- ⅓ yard (30.5cm) black-and-white striped quilt cotton for outer border
- 44" x 52" (1.1 x 1.3m) batting
- 44" x 52" (1.1 x 1.3m) backing
- 184" (4.7m) binding*
  *For an angled binding design, the strips were cut on the bias of the black-and-white striped print.

Cutting

From the assorted character prints
    10 star block center squares, 4½" (11.4cm)
From each of eight different solids
    5 star block squares (40 total), 3" (7.6cm)
From cream quilt cotton
    40 star block squares, 3" (7.6cm)
    40 star block squares, 2½" (6.4cm)

From black quilt cotton
    4 inner border strips, 1½" (3.8cm) x WOF
From black-and-white stripe
    4 outer border strips, 2½" (6.4cm) x WOF
From binding
    2¼" (5.7cm) strips cut on the bias and joined to equal 184" (4.7m) of binding

Making the Half-Square Triangles

1 Draw a straight line from corner to corner on the wrong side of 40 cream 3" (7.6cm) squares.

2 Place a solid-color square wrong sides together with the marked cream square. Stitch ¼" (6mm) to either side of the drawn line. Refer to "HSTs and Chain Stitching Blocks" on page 30.

3 Using a rotary cutter and straight edge, cut directly on the drawn line to yield two half-square triangles (HSTs).

4 Using a rotary cutter and square ruler, trim your HSTs to 2½" (6.4cm). The center line between colors should run perfectly diagonal from one corner to the other.

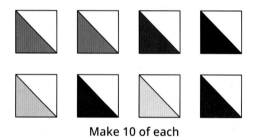

Make 10 of each

5 Repeat for the remaining colored squares. You should have 10 of each cream/color combination for a total of 80 HSTs.

6 To make joining the squares easier and result in a flatter block, press the seam allowances for the orange, brown, light blue, and blue HSTs toward the cream side. Press the seam allowances for the yellow, red, green, and black HSTs to the color side.

Making the Blocks

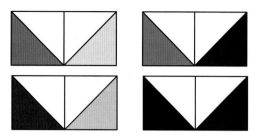

1 Before laying out your rows, join a cream/yellow square to a cream/orange square; a cream/green square to a cream/blue square; a cream/light blue square to a cream/red square; and a cream/black to a cream/brown square.

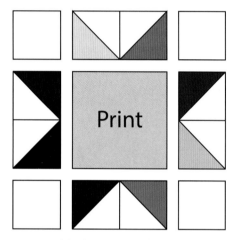

2 Lay out your block pieces as follows, making sure the colored triangles are facing as indicated:

   Row 1: cream square, cream/yellow/orange unit, cream square

   Row 2: cream/brown/black unit, character print square, cream/red/light blue unit

   Row 3: cream square, cream/blue/green unit, cream square

Tip

When you press your seams in alternate directions on HSTs and flat in your HST unit joins, your blocks lie flatter. **Note:** This is the back side of the block.

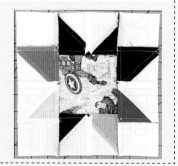

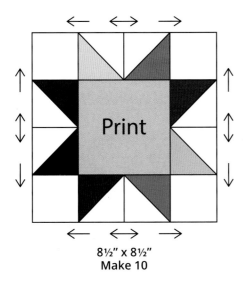

8½" x 8½"
Make 10

3 Join the units in each row, pressing the seam allowances as indicted by the arrows. Join the rows together.

5 Repeat to make 10 blocks total, each 8½" (21.6cm) square.

Building the Quilt

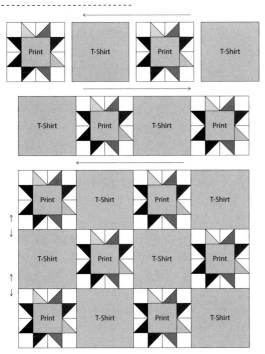

1 Lay out and alternate your T-shirt blocks and star blocks, as shown in the quilt diagram. You will have four blocks across and five blocks down.

2 Stitch the blocks in each row together. Press the seam allowance on rows 1, 3, and 5 to the left and on rows 2 and 4 to the right.

3 Stitch the rows together, pressing the seam allowances open.

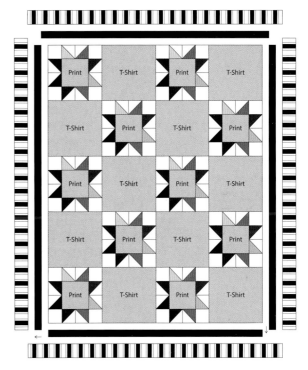

4 Join a 1½" (3.8cm) x WOF strip to each side. Trim the strips at the top and bottom even with the quilt. Press open. Join a 1½" (3.8cm) x WOF strip to the top and bottom, press, and trim the strips even with the width of the quilt. The quilt with inner border attached should measure 34½" x 42½" (87.6 x 108cm). Press the seam allowance toward the borders.

5 Following the same techniques in step 4, join the 2½" (6.4cm) x WOF border strips to the inner borders, trim, and press to finish the quilt top. Press the seam allowance toward the inner borders.

6 Layer with batting and backing. Quilt as desired. The design shown was professionally quilted with a star pattern on a long arm machine.

7 Bind with 2¼" (5.7cm) wide binding cut on the bias from your black-and-white stripe.

Fixing a Duplicate Block with Color

Quilt done, long arming finished, and binding ready—then you notice. Slapping your forehead, you think, "How in the world did I do that?" Even after puzzling over your blocks around 20 times to get the best arrangement, you somehow ended up with two very similar prints, one on top of the other. If your culprit print has a light- or medium-hue background, turn to fabric markers for the win!

Pick one that suits your design, test it on the fabric in question to see if you like the results, and then carefully color away. If your quilting thread is high contrast, very carefully work around it with a finer tip. You can see how changing the white background on the bottom square gives it a different feel, so the "mistake" isn't nearly as obvious.

I used the B1 Pastel Blue Art Alternative Illustration Marker. These markers come in lots of colors, don't bleed, and have a blunt tip on one end and a pointed tip on the other. Test color and implement on exact fabric scraps to make sure you like the results before you proceed. I even washed my sample to test the colorfastness.

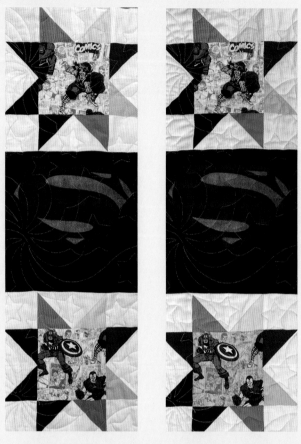

These character prints (left) are too close together for my liking; after adding blue to the background (right), they now look distinct from one another.

Template Quilting Star Pattern

Photocopy at 200%

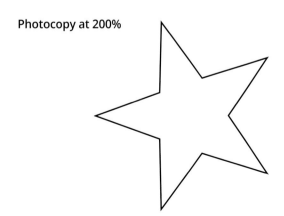

1 Using transparent tape, tape on the adjoining patches around the block to be colored. Although the marker shown doesn't bleed, you don't want to accidently get ink on anything other than your intended block.

2 Carefully color on the background of your print, using the fine tip to mark next to any stitching lines and applying an equal density of color. Once you are pleased, remove the tape.

3 To set the dye, place an iron on a cotton setting directly on top of the colored block and press.

Kid's Character Wall Hanging

What happens when one of your child's favorite tees can't be cut to suit the design you've chosen? You could redesign your quilt, but that's a challenge with just one wonky size. You could cut through part of the design, which works nicely for some graphics, but isn't ideal for every T-shirt. Or you could combine your oddly sized block with scraps to create a coordinated wall hanging.

To make the design shown, you'll need one extra star block from the Kid's Character T-Shirt Quilt. Quilt was lightly quilted on a standard machine using the star template (see page 64).

Finished Size: 20½" x 17½" (52.1 x 44.5cm)
¼" seam allowance throughout

Materials

- 1 T-shirt
  Unfinished block size: One 9½" x 8½" (24.1 x 21.6cm)
- One 8½" x 8½" (21.6 x 21.6cm) star block (refer to materials and instructions on page 60)
- One 6" x 18" (15.2 x 45.7cm) character print or two 6" x 9" (15.2 x 22.9cm) pieces in different prints
- ⅓ yard (30.5cm) black-and-white stripe quilting cotton
- 24" x 21" (61 x 53.3cm) backing fabric
- 24" x 21" (61 x 53.3cm) batting
- 10½" (26.7cm) 100% cotton fusible interfacing
- 86" (2.2m) of binding (3 strips)

Cutting

From character print
    1 rectangle, 5½" x 8½" (14 x 21.6cm)
    1 rectangle, 4½" x 8½" (11.4 x 21.6cm)
From black-and-white stripe
    4 border strips, 18" x 4½" (45.7 x 11.4cm)
    1 hanging tab strip, 15" x 2½" (38.1 x 6.4cm)

Instructions

1 Prepare your T-shirt with interfacing as described on page 22. Cut your T-shirt block to 9½" x 8½" (24.1 x 21.6cm).

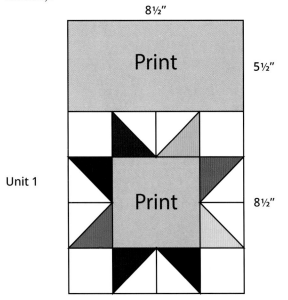

8½"

Print

5½"

Unit 1

Print

8½"

2 Stitch the 5½" x 8½" (14 x 21.6cm) character print to the top of the star block. This creates unit 1. Press.

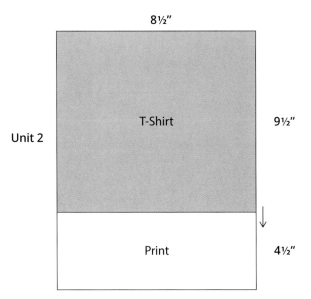

8½"

T-Shirt

9½"

Unit 2

Print

4½"

3 Stitch the 4½" x 8½" (11.4 x 21.6cm) character print to the bottom of the T-shirt block. This creates unit 2. Press from the back side or use a pressing cloth so as to not damage the T-shirt design.

Unit 1 (RS)

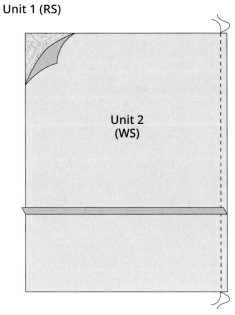

Unit 2
(WS)

4 Place unit 1 right sides together with unit 2, and stitch down the right-hand side. Open and press seam open. This is your wall hanging center. It should measure 16½" x 13½" (41.9 x 34.3cm).

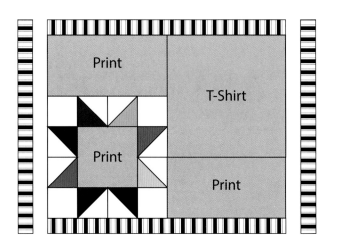

Print

T-Shirt

Print

Print

5 Apply border strips to the top and bottom of the center. Press open and trim the ends even with the center. Apply remaining two border strips to the sides, press open, and trim ends even with the top and bottom strips.

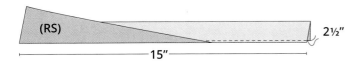

(RS)   2½"

|———————— 15" ————————|

6 With the 15" x 2½" (38.1 x 6.4cm) stripe fabric, fold the 15" (38.1cm) side in half, long raw edge to long raw edge, and press. Stitch along the long raw edges with a ¼" (6mm) seam allowance to create a tube.

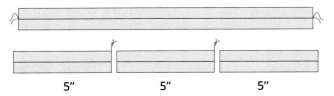

5"   5"   5"

7 Turn the tube right side out. Press your tube so that the seam line is in the center of one side (the back). Cut into three 5" (12.7cm) pieces for your tabs.

8 Fold each tab piece in half and press. Set aside.

9 Layer the quilt top, batting, and backing, and quilt as desired. See page 33 for technique of quilting with a template.

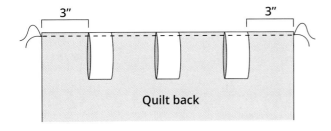

3"   3"

Quilt back

10 Before binding, position the three hanging tabs: centered, 3" (7.6cm) from each side, and raw ends aligned with top raw edge on the quilt back. Pin and baste with a ¼" (6mm) seam.

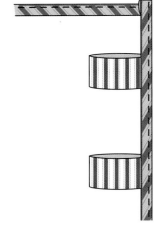

11 Cut binding strips on the bias (vertically across the fabric). Apply binding on the wrong side first. Then fold to right side, press, and edge stitch to secure, folding tabs up as you stitch.

Rectangle-Block T-Shirt Quilt

Long arm quilted by The Little Red Quilt House, Medina County, Ohio

Often, T-shirt logos are much wider than they are long. This design works with five T-shirt blocks cut into rectangles rather than squares and paired with 10" (25.4cm) finished blocks.

Finished Size: 42½" x 61½" (1.1 x 1.6m)
¼" (6mm) seam allowance (unless otherwise noted)

Materials

- 5 T-shirts
  Unfinished block size: Five 10½" x 14½" (26.7 x 36.8cm)
- ⅞ yard (80cm) stripe fabric for sashing and borders
- ⅛ yard (11.4cm) each of three turquoise prints
- ⅓ yard (30.5cm) yellow solid fabric for blocks
- ⅓ yard (30.5cm) navy print fabric for blocks
- ½ yard (45.7cm) light gray print fabric for blocks
- 1¾ yards (1.6m) 100% cotton fusible interfacing
- 2⅔ yards (2.4m) backing fabric
- 218" (5.5m) of binding (6 strips)

Cutting

From turquoise print A
    4 block squares, 4" (10.2cm)
    16 block squares, 3" (7.6cm)
From turquoise print B
    4 block squares, 4" (10.2cm)
    16 block squares, 3" (7.6cm)
From turquoise print C
    2 block squares, 4" (10.2cm)
    8 block squares, 3" (7.6cm)
From yellow solid
    20 block squares, 3½" (8.9cm)

From navy print
    20 block squares, 3½" (8.9cm)
From light gray print
    40 block squares, 3½" (8.9cm)
    20 block squares, 3½" (8.9cm), cut
       diagonal to yield 40 triangles
From stripe
    10 sashing strips, 10½" x 2½"
      (26.7 x 6.4cm)
    4 sashing strips, 38½" x 2½"
      (97.8 x 6.4cm)

Making the T-Shirt Sections

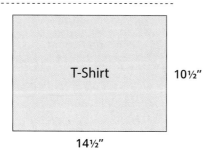

T-Shirt

10½"

14½"

1 Prepare your five T-shirts with interfacing as described on page 22. Center the logos and cut five 10½" x 14½" (26.7 x 36.8cm) rectangles.

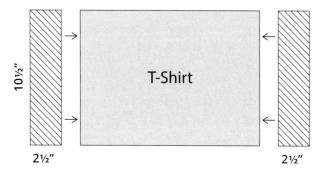

10½"

T-Shirt

2½"   2½"

2 Join the short sides of each T-shirt rectangle with a 10½" x 2½" (26.7 x 6.4cm) sashing strip. Press the seam allowance toward the T-shirt block.

Making the Blocks

3½" x 3½"
Prepare 40

1 Draw a diagonal line from corner to corner on the wrong side of 40 gray 3½" (8.9cm) squares.

2 Place each square right sides together with the 20 yellow squares and 20 navy print squares, marked side facing you. Stitch ¼" (6mm) to each side of the marked line.

3" x 3"   3" x 3"
Make 40   Make 40

3 Using a ruler and rotary cutter, cut the stitched squares apart on the marked line, yielding 40 gray/navy HSTs and 40 gray/yellow HSTs. Press the seams open. Trim each HST to 3" (7.6cm) square.

  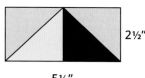

2½"

5½"
Make 40

4 Pair one yellow/gray HST right sides together with one navy/gray HST; arrange so the gray sections face out. Stitch. Press seam open. Repeat to make 40 units.

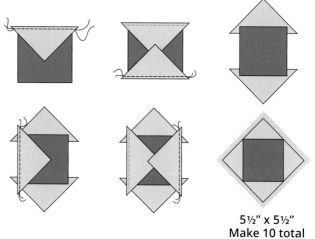

5½" x 5½"
Make 10 total

5 Center the long edge of a gray triangle on the straight edge of one 4" (10.2cm) turquoise print square. Stitch with a ¼" (6mm) seam allowance. Press with seam allowance toward the triangle. Add a second gray triangle on the opposite side of the square, stitch, and press open. Repeat with two more gray triangles, working one side at a time. Press and trim to 5½" (14cm) square. You should have a ¼" (6mm) seam allowance extending beyond each point of the centered square. Repeat to make 10 total units: four of prints A and B, and two of print C.

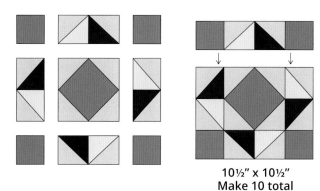

10½" x 10½"
Make 10 total

6 Position your block pieces as shown. Match the turquoise print in the block center with the four 3" (7.6cm) turquoise blocks in the corners. Join each row, then join the three rows to complete your 10½" (26.7cm) block. Repeat to make 10 blocks.

7 Join matching blocks to each side of the sashing strips on the T-shirt sections. Press the seam allowance toward the blocks.

NOTE: If you have an order in which you want your T-shirts to be placed, make sure to join the blocks to the T-shirt units so that print A is in the first and last row, print B is the second and fourth row, and print C is the center row.

Building the Quilt

1 Lay out your prepared T-shirt rows so that print A is in rows 1 and 5, print B is in rows 2 and 4, and print C is in row 3. Refer to the quilt diagram on page 75.

2 Join a 38½" x 2½" (97.8 x 6.4cm) stripe sashing strip to the bottom of rows 1–4. Do not join a sashing row to the bottom of row 5. Join the top of each row to the sashing strip from the previous row to complete the quilt center.

3 Press the quilt center. Measure the sides and cut two side border strips at the length with a width of 2½" (6.4cm), approximately 58½" x 2½" (148.6 x 6.4cm). Join to the quilt sides. Even up the side border strips in line with the top and bottom of the quilt if needed. Press.

4 Cut top and bottom border strips like step 3, but with side borders attached; measures approximately 42½" x 2½" (108 x 6.4cm). Join to the top and bottom of the quilt to complete the top.

5 Layer the quilt top, batting, and backing. Quilt and bind as desired.

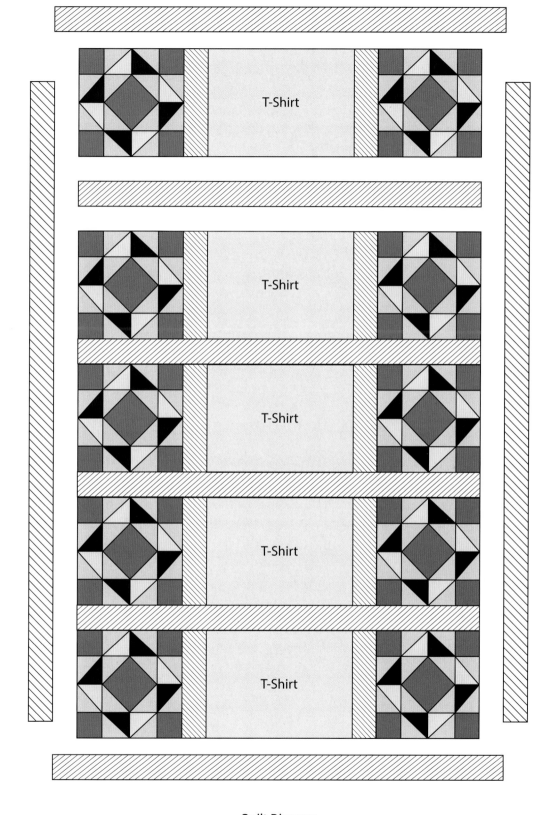

Quilt Diagram

T-Shirt Tote for a Cause

There is a fundraising-for-a-cause event nearly every weekend. Whatever that cause may be, whether it involves running, walking, biking, or another sports competition, a guarantee for each and every one is a T-shirt. This tote for a cause uses four or five T-shirts, has three outside pockets, including one with elastic for a water bottle, and an optional zipper top panel to keep everything secured inside. This is perfect for volunteering, hospital visits, or when you're on the go!

Finished Size: 15½" x 18" x 4½" (39.4 x 45.7 x 11.4cm)
¼" (6mm) seam allowance (unless otherwise noted)

Materials

- 4–5 T-shirts
  Unfinished block sizes:
  One 12½" x 11" (31.8 x 28cm) for front pocket
  One 12½" x 13" (31.8 x 33cm) for back pocket
  One 16" x 5" (40.6 x 12.7cm) for side piece*
  One 12½" x 8" (31.8 x 20.3cm) for
    bottle pocket
  *In this example, two logos were joined to
    reach this length
- ⅔ yard (60cm) small floral print (A) for bag
  front, back, bottom, and sides
- ⅜ yard (34.3cm) turquoise print (B) for front
  pocket lining and bag bottom
- ⅜ yard (34.3cm) pink/orange animal print (C)
  for back pocket lining
- ⅜ yard (34.3cm) large floral print (D) for
  binding and bottle pocket lining
- ½ yard (45.7cm) light pink print (E) for
  bag straps
- 1⅜ yards (1.3m) fusible foam batting (I used
  Flex-Foam 1-Sided Fusible)
- 1¾ yards (1.6m) heavy-weight interfacing
- 12" x ⅜" (30.5 x 1cm) elastic
- Optional: ¾" (1.9cm) wide sew-in hook-and-
  loop fastener (I used VELCRO®)
- Optional: ½ yard (45.7cm) zipper (I used
  Dream Big Creations in pink polka dot)
- Optional: #3 zipper pull

Cutting

From print A
  2 front and back rectangles, 19" x 16" (48.3 x 40.6cm)
  1 side rectangle, 5" x 16" (12.7 x 40.6cm)
From print B
  1 front pocket lining rectangle, 12½" x 13" (31.8 x 33cm)
  1 bag bottom rectangle, 5" x 19" (12.7 x 48.3cm)
From print C
  1 back pocket lining rectangle, 12½" x 15 (31.8 x 38.1cm)
  Optional: 2 top zipper band strips, 4½" x 19" (11.4 x 48.3cm)
  Optional: 2 zipper end rectangles, 3" x 5 ¼" (7.6 x 13.3cm)
From print D
  1 bottle pocket lining rectangle, 8" x 14" (20.3 x 35.6cm)
From print E
  3 strap strips, 4" (10.2cm) x WOF, join and cut for two
    4" x 60" (10.2 x 152.4cm) strips
  2 front and back lining rectangles, 19" x 16" (48.3 x 40.6cm)
  2 side lining rectangles, 5" x 16" (12.7 x 40.6cm)
  1 bag bottom lining rectangle, 5" x 19" (12.7 x 48.3cm)
From fusible foam batting:
  2 front and back rectangles, 19" x 16" (48.3 x 40.6cm)
  2 side rectangles, 5" x 16" (12.7 x 40.6cm)
  1 bag bottom rectangle, 5" x 19" (12.7 x 48.3cm)
From heavy-weight interfacing
  Optional: 2 top zipper band strips, 2" x 18½" (5.1 x 47cm)
  2 strap strips, 1½" x 60" (3.8 x 152.4cm)

Preparing the T-Shirts

1 Prepare your T-shirts with interfacing as described on page 22.

2 Cut T-shirts to the following sizes:
  Front pocket: 12½" x 11" (31.8 x 28cm)
  Back pocket: 12½" x 13" (31.8 x 33cm)
  Side piece: 5" x 16" (12.7 x 40.6cm)
  Bottle pocket 8" x 12½" (20.3 x 31.8cm)

Making the Front & Back Pockets

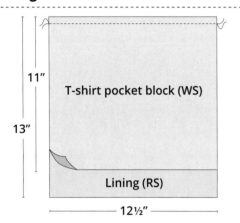

1 Place front pocket lining piece right sides together with prepared front pocket T-shirt block. Stitch across the top with ⅜" (1cm) seam allowance.

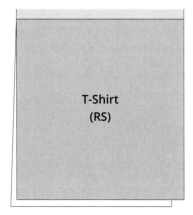

2 Press the seam allowance up and fold the lining piece around to the back so the T-shirt block and lining are wrong sides together. Press again so that you've created a faux binding at the top of your pocket piece.

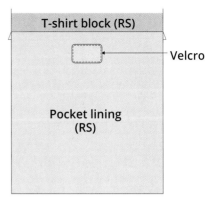

Optional: If you'd like a hook-and-loop closure on your pocket, cut a 1"–2" (2.4–5.1cm) strip. Separate and pin the soft side to the center of your pocket lining piece, just below the faux binding. Separate the pocket layer from the lining and stitch around the edges of the square to join it to the lining fabric only.

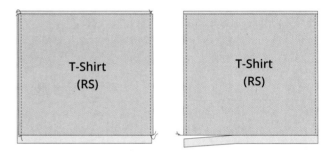

3 Place the pocket and lining wrong sides together. Baste through all layers with ¼" (6mm) seam allowance down both sides. Trim the excess lining fabric at the bottom even with the bottom edge of the T-shirt block. Finished pocket piece should be 12½" x 11 (31.8 x 28cm).

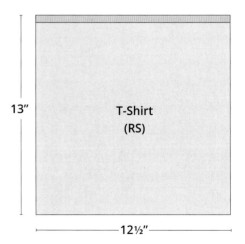

4 Repeat steps 1–3 for the back pocket. Finished back pocket piece should be 12½" x 13" (31.8 x 33cm).

Making the Bottle Pocket

1 Place the bottle T-shirt block and the bottle lining pieces right sides together. Stitch across the top with a ⅜" (1cm) seam allowance as you did for the front and back pockets.

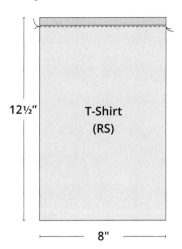

2 Press the seam allowance up, and fold the lining piece around to the back so the T-shirt block and lining are wrong sides together. Press again so that you've created a faux binding at the top of your pocket piece.

3 From the front, stitch-in-the-ditch of the faux band at the top to create a casing for the elastic.

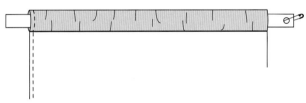

4 Feed a 12" (30.5cm) long strip of elastic through the created casing using a safety pin or bodkin. Baste the lining down one side of the pocket with a ¼" (6mm) seam allowance, catching the end of the elastic on that side. Stitch back and forth over the elastic once or twice to secure.

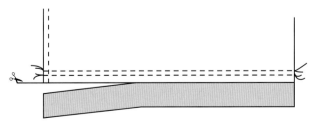

5 Trim off the excess lining fabric at the bottom of the bottle T-shirt block and run two gathering threads at ¼" (6mm) and ½" (1.3cm) across the bottom.

WATCH
HOW TO MACHINE
SEW THE STITCH

Preparing the Bag Pieces

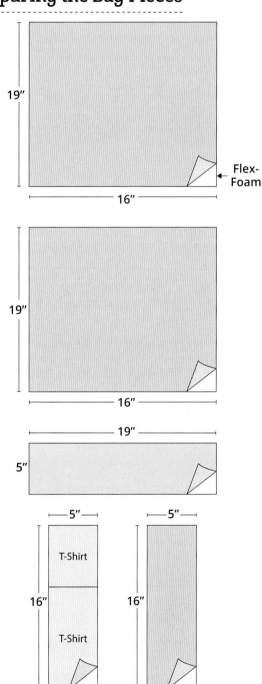

1 Apply the fusible foam batting to all the bag pieces: front, back, side, bottom, and T-shirt side block.

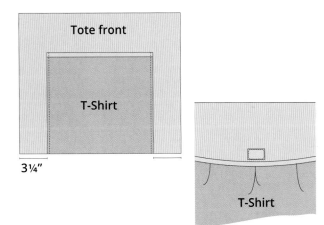

3¼"

2 Place the front pockets on the front bag pieces, centered and even with the bottom edges. You should have 3¼" (8.3cm) flat fabric on each side of the pocket placement. Stitch down both sides and across the bottom with a ¼" (6mm) seam allowance.

Optional: Position and stitch the hook side of your hook-and-loop fastener on the body of the tote. Repeat with the prepared back and back pocket.

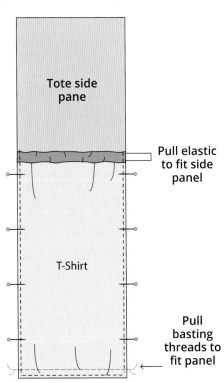

3 Place the prepared bottle pocket block on the prepared fabric side piece so that the left sides and bottoms are aligned. Stitch down the side to secure.

4 Gather the top of the pocket piece by pulling the end of the elastic until it fits the 5" (12.7cm) width; pin in place. Now gather the pocket bottom by pulling bobbin threads of basting stitches to gather it to the 5" (12.7cm) width. Position most of the gathers in the center of the pocket; pin. Stitch down the side and across the bottom through all layers. Stitch over the elastic at the top two or three times to secure.

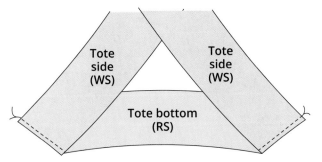

5 Right sides together, pin and stitch the side panels to either side of the prepared bottom panel using a ¼" (6mm) seam allowance. Set unit aside.

Making the Handles

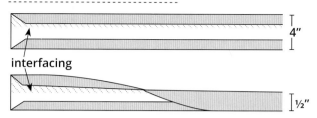

interfacing

4"

½"

1 Fuse a 1½" x 60" (3.8 x 152.4cm) strip of heavyweight interfacing down the wrong side of each 4" x 60" (10.2 x 152.4cm) strip. Place interfacing ½" (1.3cm) away from edge (will be placed inside seam allowance).

2 Working with one strap at a time, fold under ½" (1.3cm) seam allowance down both long sides and press. Then fold the strip in half wrong sides together, aligning the folded-under edges. To secure for edge stitching, glue-baste the open side of the strap. Repeat for the remaining strap. Straps should finish 1½" (3.8cm) wide.

3a Position a strap on the front tote panel so that the ends are at the bottom of the tote edge and the strap is centered over the raw edges of the attached pocket block. Make sure to not twist the strap. The glue-basted side should be facing inward. Pin and baste across the lower edge.

T-Shirt

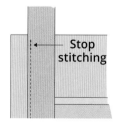

Stop stitching

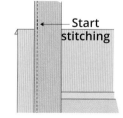

Start stitching

3b Edge stitch the strips from the bottom of the tote, stopping ½" (3.81cm) from the top edge of the tote panel front. Backstitch and clip the threads. Fold under the tote top to separate the strap from the tote. Keeping the top of the tote out of the stitch line, continue edge stitching on the strap only.

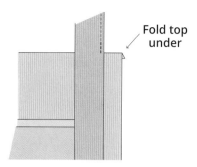

Fold top under

3c When you come to the opposite side of the tote, fold under the tote top ½" (3.81cm). Edge stitch the strip to ½" (3.81cm) past the tote top (with the back folded out of the way). Backstitch. Then unfold the tote top and finish stitching the strip to the body of the tote and to the bottom. Repeat with the inside edge of the strap. Then repeat with the back panel and the second strap.

Building the Bag

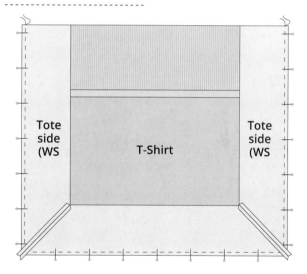

Tote side (WS

T-Shirt

Tote side (WS

1 Working one side at a time, wrong sides together, pin the side/bottom unit to the tote front, aligning the lower edge of the unit so that the side/bottom joins are ¼" (6mm) from each side edge. Beginning at the center bottom, stitch to ¼" (6mm) before the corner, leave the needle down, pivot the bag, and sew up the side to the top. Return to the bottom and sew the remaining side.

2 Using the same process as step 1, join the bag back to the opposite side of the side/bottom unit.

Optional: Zipper Top

1 If using zipper by the yard, place zipper pull on zipper and trim tape to 18½" (47cm). If using a standard zipper, trim off the end so that zipper measures 18½" (47cm).

2 Fold fabric rectangles to finish ends of zipper in half lengthwise. Fold raw edges in to meet the center and press in half. Strips should be ¾" (1.9cm) wide.

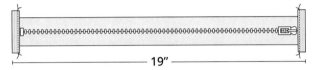

3 Place folded rectangles from step 2 over ½" (1.3cm) of zipper ends and topstitch. Unit should be 19" (48.3cm) long.

4 Fold zipper band pieces in half lengthwise, wrong sides together, and press. Insert heavy-weight interfacing strip so it is against the fold and fuse.

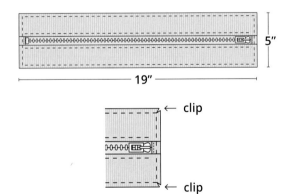

5 Place the folded edge of the zipper band piece approximately ⅛" (3mm) from the zipper teeth. Edge stitch the band to the zipper from tab to tab. Repeat on the opposite side with the remaining band. Trim the zipper panel so that it measures 5" (12.7cm) wide with the zipper centered. Staystitch all the way around the zipper panel with ¼" (6mm) seam allowance. Clip diagonally at all four corners just to the stitching line. Set unit aside.

Lining

1 Join the sides and bottom lining pieces, then join the front and back lining pieces to the side/back unit as you did for the outer bag. Press the side/back seam allowances away from the body of the bag toward the sides.

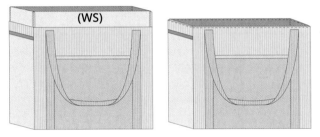

2 Turn lining inside out and insert into bag, aligning the seams. Pin, nesting the seams at the sides. Stitch around the top with a ¼" (6mm) seam allowance.

3 Optional zipper top:

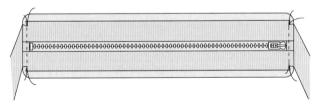

3a Pin one end of the zipper top panel to one end of the tote top, wrong sides together. Match the ¼" (6mm) seamline on the zipper panel to the side seams of the tote. Pin and stitch just from one side seam to the other so that you have ¼" (6mm) unstitched on each side of the zipper top panel. Repeat for the other side.

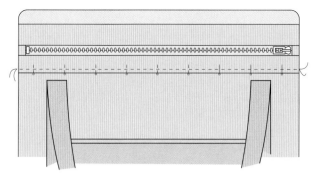

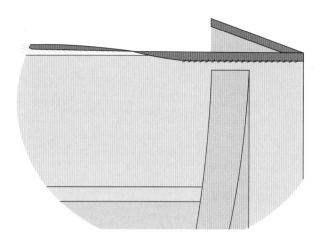

3b Pin the remaining long sides of the zipper panel to the top sides of the tote, wrong sides together. Stitch to attach, starting your stitch line at the center top of the tote and working toward the end. Stop and secure stitching at the corner. Return to the center and stitch in the other direction. Unzip the zipper to give the top more give, and repeat for the opposite side.

Binding

1 Following the same technique used to bind a quilt, create 54" x 2¼" (137.2 x 5.7cm) binding from print D. Press strip in half lengthwise.

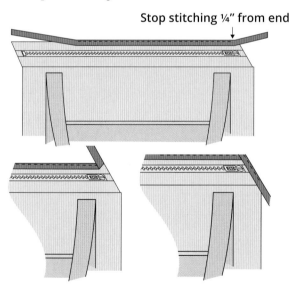

Stop stitching ¼" from end

2 Leaving a 6" (15.2cm) tail, begin stitching the binding strip to the top of the tote slightly left of center. When you come to the first corner, stop stitching ¼" (6mm) from the edge, secure stitching, and create your corner; refer to "Binding Quilt Edges" on page 38 if needed.

3 Continue binding around the back in the same manner, joining binding ends as you would on a quilt. Once you've machine stitched the binding to the inside edge of the tote top, fold it around to the front side and hand stitch in place to secure. Use tiny stitches and matching thread.

NOTE: If you don't add the zipper top, you could also machine stitch the binding in place with an edge stitch.

4 To complete and strengthen your straps, stitch a square with an X through each strap just under the binding, being careful not to catch your zipper top in your stitch line.

Two-Block T-Shirt Quilt

Quilted by The Little Red Quilt House, Medina County, Ohio

Two 10" (25.4cm) blocks, the Bento Box and a simple strip block, lend a masculine touch to this football-themed design. As shown, the design incorporates seven tees, but you could add four more by swapping out the strip-pieced blocks and still have a nice touch of patchwork in the center.

Finished Size: 48½" x 60½" (1.2 x 1.5m)
¼" seam allowance throughout

Materials

- 7 T-shirts
  Unfinished block size: Seven 12½" x 12½" (31.8 x 31.8cm)
- ½ yard (45.7cm) black print for blocks
- ½ yard (45.7cm) light gray print for blocks
- ½ yard (45.7cm) red print (A) for blocks
- ⅓ yard (30.5cm) white print for blocks and inner border
- 1¾ yards (1.6m) red print (B) for outer border
- 2⅞ yards (2.6m) 100% cotton fusible interfacing
- 3¼ yards (3m) backing fabric
- 228" (5.8m) of binding (6 strips)

Cutting

From white print
  2 inner border strips, 62" x 2" (157.5 x 5.1cm)
  2 inner border strips, 42" x 2" (106.7 x 5.1cm)
From red print (B)
  2 outer border strips, 65" x 3¼" (165.1 x 8.3cm)
  2 outer border strips, 47" x 3¼" (119.4 x 8.3cm)
For Bento Box blocks:
From light gray print
  8 strips, 2½" x 5¼" (6.4 x 13.3cm)
  16 strips, 2½" x 4½" (6.4 x 11.4cm)
  8 strips, 2½" x 6½" (6.4 x 16.5cm)

From red (A) and white prints
  4 strips, 2½" x 5¼" (6.4 x 13.3cm)
  8 strips, 2½" x 4½" (6.4 x 11.4cm)
  8 strips, 2½" x 6½" (6.4 x 16.5cm)
From black print
  4 strips, 2½" x 5¼" (6.4 x 13.3cm)
  8 strips, 2½" x 4½" (6.4 x 11.4cm)
For strip blocks:
From red (A), gray, white, and black prints
  8 strips, 2" x 11" (5.1 x 28cm)

Preparing the T-Shirts

1 Prepare your T-shirts with interfacing as described on page 22.

2 Center and cut out seven 12½" (31.8cm) square blocks from your prepared T-shirts.

Making the Bento Box Blocks

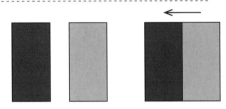

1 Right sides together, join a light gray and red 2½" x 5¼" (6.4 x 13.3cm) strip along one long side. Press the seam toward the red rectangle. Square the unit to 5" x 4½" (12.7 x 11.4cm).

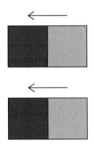

2 Cut the unit from step 1 into two 2½" x 4½" (6.4 x 11.4cm) units with red/gray squares.

3 Join a light gray 2½" x 4½" (6.4 x 11.4cm) strip to the top of one unit from step 2, making sure the red square is to the left. Press the seam allowance toward the red/gray unit. Repeat for the second unit.

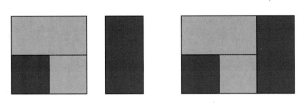

4 Join a red 2½" x 4½" (6.4 x 11.4cm) strip to the right of the unit from step 3. Press the seam allowance toward the red strip. Repeat for the second unit.

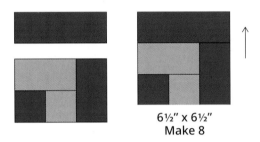

6½" x 6½"
Make 8

5 Join a red 2½" x 6½" (6.4 x 16.5cm) strip to the top of the unit from step 4. Press the seam toward the red strip. Repeat for the second unit and set these two units aside.

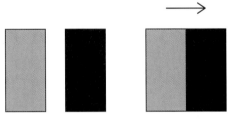

6 Right sides together, join a light gray and black 2½" x 5¼" (6.4 x 13.3cm) strip along one long side. Press the seam toward the black rectangle. Square the unit to 5" x 4½" (12.7 x 11.4cm).

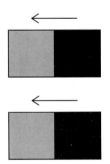

7 Cut the unit from step 6 into two 2½" x 4½" (6.4 x 11.4cm) units with gray/black squares.

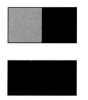

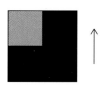

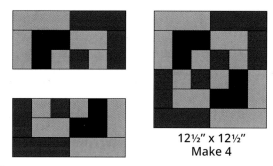

8 Join a black 2½" x 4½" (6.4 x 11.4cm) strip to the bottom of one unit from step 7, making sure the black square is to the right. Press the seam allowance toward the gray/black unit. Repeat for the second unit.

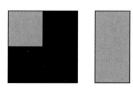

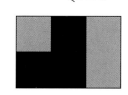

12½" x 12½"
Make 4

12 Join the top and bottom units together to complete the 12½" (31.8cm) square block. Press the seam open.

13 Repeat to make four Bento Box blocks.

9 Join a light gray 2½" x 4½" (6.4 x 11.4cm) strip to the right of the unit from step 8. Press the seam allowance toward the black strip. Repeat for the second unit.

Making the Strip Blocks

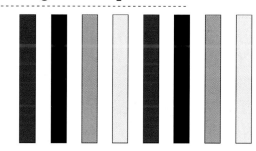

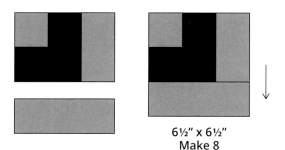

6½" x 6½"
Make 8

1 Order your strips as shown so that the white print is strip 4 and 8.

10 Join a light gray 2½" x 6½" (6.4 x 16.5cm) strip to the bottom of the unit from step 9. Press the seam toward the light gray strip. Repeat for the second unit.

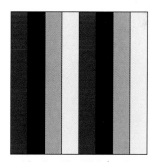

12½" x 12½" Make 4

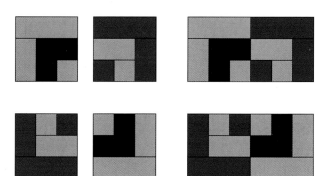

11 Lay out all four units, making sure that each unit is oriented as shown. Join the two top units and press the seam open. Repeat for the two bottom units.

2 Stitch the strips together in order one by one using a ¼" (6mm) seam allowance. Make sure your strips are an accurate 1½" (3.8cm) once joined together; the outer strips should measure 1¾" (4.4cm) to allow for the outer seam allowance. Press the seam allowances toward the darker fabrics. Once joined, trim your strip block to 12½" (31.8cm) square.

3 Repeat to make four strip blocks.

Building the Quilt Top

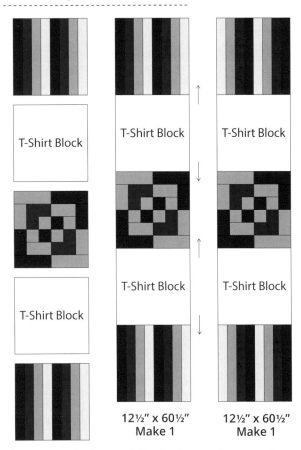

12½" x 60½"
Make 1

12½" x 60½"
Make 1

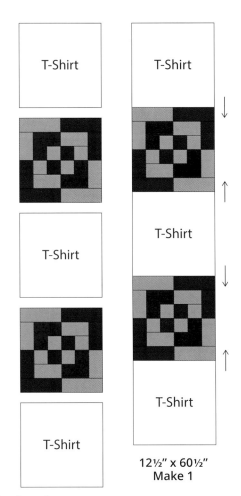

12½" x 60½"
Make 1

1 Arrange the first and third column of your quilt top:

1a Column 1: A strip block with the white strip on the right side, a T-shirt block, a Bento Box block with the red L shape on the lower-left corner, a second T-shirt block, and a second strip block with the white strip on the right side. Join the units from top to bottom. Press the seam allowance away from the T-shirt blocks.

1b Repeat for column 3; however, make sure that the white strip on your strip block is on the left side as shown.

2 Arrange the middle column: A T-shirt block, a Bento Box block with the red L shape on the lower left-corner, a second T-shirt block, a second Bento Box block, and a third T-shirt block. Press the seam allowances away from the T-shirt blocks.

3 Join the columns.

4 For the inner border, join the white print 62" x 2" (157.5 x 5.1cm) strips to the sides of the quilt. Press the seam allowance toward the quilt and trim off any excess fabric at the top or bottom in line with the quilt edges. Repeat, joining the white print 42" x 2" (106.7 x 5.1cm) strips on top and bottom.

5 For the outer border, join the red print (B) 65" x 3¼" (165.1 x 8.3cm) strips to the sides of the inner border and trim off any excess fabric at top or bottom in line with the quilt edges. Press the seam allowance toward the outer border. Repeat, joining the red print (B) 47" x 3¼" (119.4 x 8.3cm) strips on top and bottom.

6 Layer with batting and backing. Quilt and bind as desired.

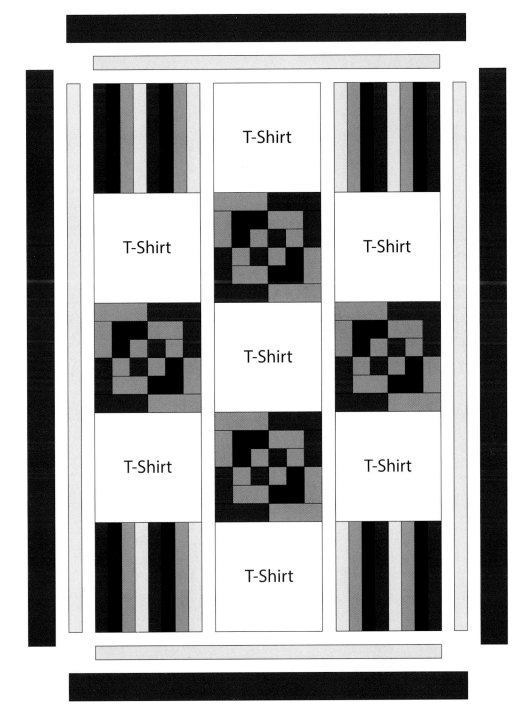

T-Shirt T-Shirt T-Shirt T-Shirt T-Shirt T-Shirt T-Shirt T-Shirt

Big Flight T-Shirt Quilt

By Kristin La Flamme

The goal for this design was to choose a block size that is not only large enough to show off T-shirt graphics, but also small enough to cut many little squares from the remainder of the shirts. It works well with overall patterns and small details, but there can also be fun surprises when a larger graphic gets cut up and rearranged. It lets you use your tees in a more abstract design that doesn't scream "T-shirt," but still holds the same memories.

Each vertical stripe is created from one shirt. The blocks are made from the large square cut from each shirt and from the main solid fabric. If you wish to substitute the solid fabric with more shirts, it is advisable to choose shirts in the same or very similar color to each other for cohesiveness.

The quilt blocks are made using the No Waste Flying Geese method for efficient use of the T-shirts. Cut and sew carefully for best results. However, as long as the geese are a consistent size, the quilt will sew together just fine. The final dimensions will be the only change. If you have more shirts, the quilt size can be enlarged by adding more rows or columns. Increase the solid fabric yardage as necessary.

Finished Size: 55" x 60" (1.4 x 1.5m)
¼" seam allowance throughout

Materials

- 5 T-shirts
  Unfinished block size:
    Five 12¼" x 12¼" (31.1 x 31.1cm)
    Sixty 6⅞" x 6⅞" (17.5 x 17.5cm)
- 1¾ yards (1.6m) red cotton fabric or color that ties the shirts together
- 7 yards (6.4m) 100% cotton fusible interfacing
- 3½ yards (3.2m) backing fabric
- 2 yards (1.8m) batting
- 240" (6.1m) of binding (6 strips)
- Reserved patches or other memorablia

Cutting

From red fabric
    10 block squares, 12¼" (31.1cm)

Preparing the T-Shirts

1 For this technique you will want to interface as much of the front and back surface area of your T-shirts as possible, as you will be cutting smaller sections. Before cutting, prepare your T-shirt fabric with interfacing, referring to page 22.

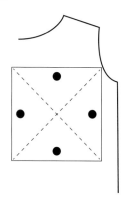

2 Cut one 12¼" (31.1cm) square block from each of five T-shirts. Center any important design elements on one side of the square (as shown by the dots in the diagram).

3 Cut twelve 6⅜" (16.2cm) squares from each of the five T-shirts for a total of 60 squares.

Making the Flying Geese Blocks

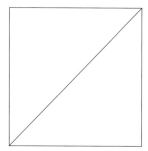

1 On the wrong side of each 6⅜" (16.2cm) T-shirt square, mark a line diagonally from one corner to the opposite corner.

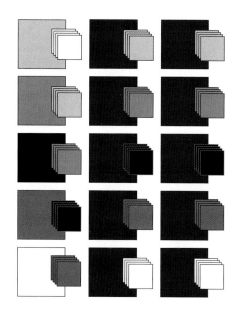

2 Pair a set of four 6⅜" (16.2cm) marked squares with each of the large T-shirt squares. The remainder of the small squares will be paired with the large red fabric squares.

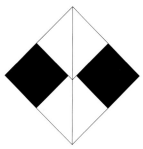

3 Choose one 12¼" (31.1cm) square and place two of the paired smaller squares, right sides together, in opposite corners. Allow the small squares to overlap in the center. Pin in place.

4 Sew a ¼" (6mm) seam on each side of the marked line. Cut on the marked line for two units.

5 Press the seam allowances open.

6 Right sides together, place each of the remaining two small squares on the large corners of the units from steps 4–5. Pin in place.

7 On each unit, sew a ¼" (6mm) seam on each side of the marked line. Cut on the marked line.

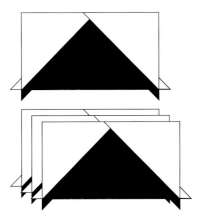

8 Press the seam allowances open. You now have four Flying Geese blocks.

9 Repeat steps 3–8 for all the 12¼" (31.1cm) squares and their paired smaller squares. You will have 60 Flying Geese blocks total. Trim to 12¼" x 6½" (31.1 x 15.2cm) if necessary.

Building the Quilt

1 Arrange your blocks in five vertical columns so the colors of the small triangles in each column match. The "geese" can point up or down. Try pairing two and rotating them 90 degrees; this is particularly effective with two blocks that use the same main color in the small triangles or when you have text you would like oriented a certain way.

2 When you are happy with the arrangement, sew the blocks together in columns. This is easier than rows if you've rotated any pairs that need to be sewn together first. Press all your seams open to reduce bulk.

3 Sew the columns together. Press seams open.

4 Quilt and bind as desired. Sew on any reserved patches.

Improv Column T-Shirt Quilt

By Jane Haworth

With this improv style—meaning every quilt ends up being unique—it doesn't really matter what size your T-shirts or logos start out, as you simply join them together or add sashing to create the column size you want, then join the columns. The nature of this T-shirt collection is that it contains a variety of logos in different styles and sizes. With this technique, adapting the width of the columns allows you to adjust the size and number of T-shirt logos you have; 30 different shirts were used in this outdoor-inspired design, some with more than one logo cut from a single tee.

Finished Size: 78" x 80" (198 x 203cm)
¼" (6mm) seam allowance (unless otherwise noted)

Materials

- 30–40 T-shirts with logos of varying sizes
  Unfinished block size: 12½" (31.8cm)
- Precut 2½" (6.4cm) strip roll in black and white or 2⅛ yards (1.9m) total of 12 different black-and-white prints
- 6 yards (5.5m) 100% cotton fusible interfacing*
  *This amount can vary depending on the number of T-shirts used
- 2½ yards (2.3m) extra-wide flannel backing fabric
- 2½ yards (2.3m) batting
- 326" (8.3m) of binding (8 strips)

Cutting

Optional: From 12 different black-and-white prints
  30 strips, 2½" (6.4cm) x WOF

Alternative to Interfacing

This quilt was pieced without using interfacing. If you don't want to work with fusible interfacing, use the cotton strips or sashing between the logos as the stabilizer. However, this is definitely a challenging approach to sewing knits, and it's recommended only experienced quilters attempt this method. The T-shirts must be very carefully cut to size, and it takes some practice to ease the knit into the strip just right. It can save money on interfacing, but there's no need to pull your hair out when there's another way! You can try this technique, or if you prefer, apply stabilizer as instructed on page 22.

The key to this method is to know the exact size cut of the T-shirt piece and cut a corresponding-sized sashing piece to attach to it. When possible, always stitch with the T-shirt fabric underneath (against the feed dogs) and fabric sashing on top, as this will ease any stretch. **NEVER** just attach sashing without it being cut to size. The T-shirt jersey will stretch, and all measurements will be off.

Making Strip Sets for Piecing

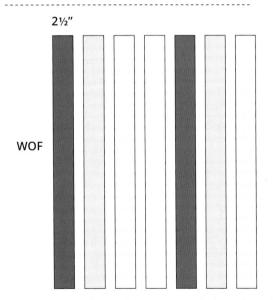

1 Join seven of your fabric strips side by side with ¼" (6mm) seam allowance. Press seam allowances to one side. (Figure 1)

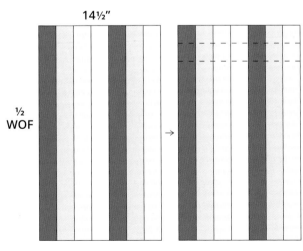

2 Cut across the center of your strip set vertically to create two equal-size units and rejoin as shown to make a strip set 28½" x 22" (72.3 x 56cm). Cut and use this as a stripy sashing in your quilt to piece your blocks to size and build your columns. I also used single strips to border and increase the dimension of my T-shirt units.

Preparing T-Shirt Units

1 Prepare your T-shirts with interfacing as described on page 22.

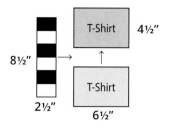

2 Cut the T-shirts into square or rectangle units, leaving about 3"–4" (7.6–10.1cm) around all four sides of the logos, if possible. For larger logos, make sure you have at least a ½" (1.3cm) border around for joining the T-shirt unit to sashing or other blocks with ¼" (6mm) seam allowance. Sort through your logo units and divide into three piles: small, medium, and large. Count and write down the number of units in each pile.

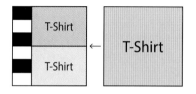

3 Determine how many large squares or logos you have—the dimensions of the large logos generally determine the width of your columns. In the featured quilt, my widest T-shirt units were 16½" (41.9cm); I also had some 14½" (36.8cm) units, so I decided that those would be my column widths. I have two 16½" (41.9cm) wide columns (columns 2 and 3) and three 14½" (36.8cm) wide columns (columns 1, 4, and 5).

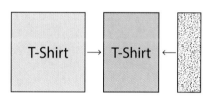

4 With 30 squares, an easy quilt layout is a 5 x 6 block pattern. Other examples could be 4 x 4 = 16 blocks, 4 x 5 = 20 blocks, 5 x 5 = 25 blocks, etc.

5 Using a large table, floor, or design wall, position your blocks in the chosen layout. As you place them, think about color placement and other design features, aiming for a balanced look.

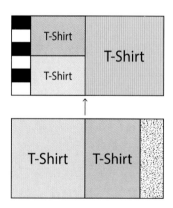

6 Having 14½" (36.8cm) and 16½" (41.9cm) wide columns means the shirts this size can be used as cut. However, many logos are cut at 12½" (31.8cm) square; the wider column size means the smaller logos are joined with a 2½" (6.4cm) sashing down each side to equal 16½" (41.2cm). At this stage, don't worry about the exact length of the columns but aim for them to be similar in length.

7 Smaller logos can be combined into larger blocks (see pages 24–25). Four small logos cut at 6½" x 6½" (16.5 x 16.5cm) will make a 12½" (31.8cm) square. Two rectangle logos cut at 6½" x 12½" (16.5 x 31.8cm) or 6½" x 14½" (16.5 x 36.8cm) will also make a block.

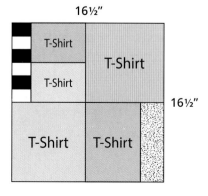

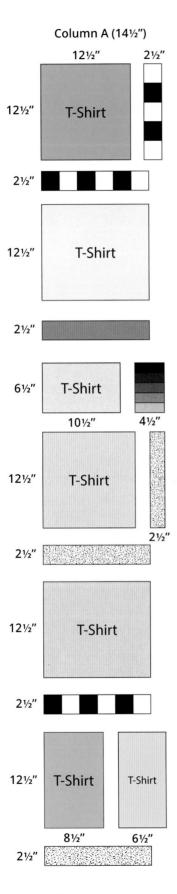

Column A (14½")

8 Using the T-shirt layout from step 5, pick up the next shirt, trim to size, cut sashing, and stitch to that sashing strip if needed to achieve your column width. Or, if sashing is not needed, trim your T-shirt to the exact width of the column. Work on one column at a time. Mix up your fabric choices. Alternate adding sashing on the left or right sides of the T-shirt; you can also add horizontal sashing pieces. Remember to cut and use your strip set as part of your sashing choices. After stitching, press the seam, press sashing away from the T-shirt, and then return the block to the layout.

9 Work across the different columns. When all the T-shirts are stitched or cut to the correct column width, it's time to measure the length of each column. As you measure each block, remember to subtract the ½" (1.3cm) seam allowance when there will be a ¼" + ¼" (6 + 6mm) seam. Write down the total length for each column.

Building the Quilt

1 Decide how long you want your quilt. It could be the average length of the columns or the longest column measurement. Where necessary, add additional sashing between the blocks so that each column finishes at the same length.

2 Pin, stitch, and join each column to its neighbor to make your completed quilt top.

3 To create a patchwork border, stitch any remaining 2½" (6.4cm) sashing pieces together. You will need two pieces for the length of your quilt. Join one to each side with a ¼" seam. Press away from the quilt top. Measure across the quilt with side borders attached and create pieced 2½" (6.4cm) border strips, one each for the top and bottom. Join and press the seam allowance away from the center.

4 Cut your backing fabric approximately 5"–6" (12.7–15.2cm) larger all around than the quilt top. Using extra-wide flannel backing means you won't have to join fabric pieces to yield a wide enough and long enough backing piece, but you certainly can choose to do so.

5 Layer your quilt with the backing fabric, batting, and quilt top. Baste as desired. To layer, I tape my backing to the floor wrong side up, layer with the batting, smooth out, and do the same with the quilt top. Baste with quilting safety pins 8" (20.3cm) apart.

6 Quilt and bind as desired. **Note:** I use free-motion quilting and stitch around the logos, color matching my thread as I go. I also stitch a simple pattern in the sashing.

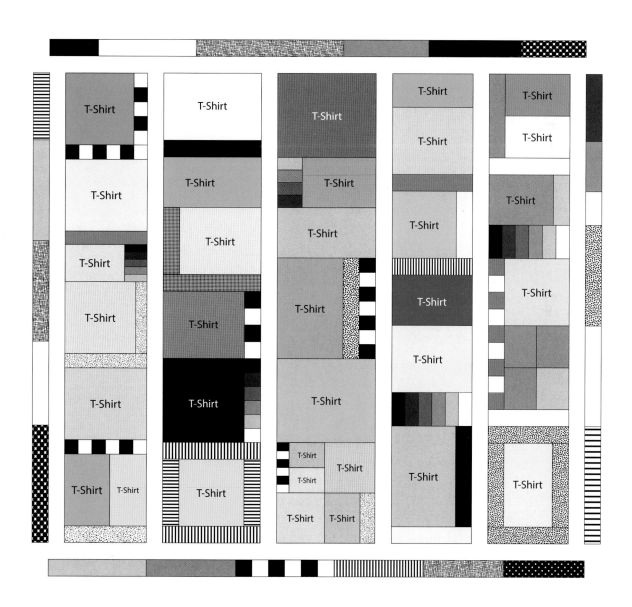

Waterfall T-Shirt Quilt

By Jill Nelson

Blocks in the Waterfall design couldn't be any easier as they are cut either from a T-shirt or from quilt fabric, no additional patchwork required. This design is like a traditional T-shirt quilt layout, combining more than 20 different T-shirt motifs with 8 solid blocks.

Approximate Finished Size: 67½" x 83½" (1.7 x 2.1m)
¼" (6mm) seam allowance (unless otherwise noted)

Materials & Tools

- 23 T-shirts
  Unfinished block sizes:
  One 12½" x 20½" (31.8 x 52.1cm)
  Eleven 12½" x 16½" (31.8 x 41.9cm)
  Nine 12½" x 12½" (31.8 x 31.8cm)
  Two 12½" x 8½" (31.8 x 21.6cm)
- 2⅔ yards (2.4m) solid-white quilt cotton
- 3½ yards (3.2m) 100% cotton fusible interfacing
- 2½ yards (2.3m) extra-wide backing
- 2½ yards (2.3m) light-weight batting, at least 75" (1.9m) wide
- 312" (7.9m) of binding (8 strips)
- Painter's tape

Cutting

From white solid
  8 Waterfall block rectangles, 8" x 12" (20.3 x 30.5cm)
  2 border strips, 4" x 78" (10.2 x 198.1cm)
  2 border strips, 2" x 70" (5.1 x 177.8cm)
From interfacing
  1 rectangle, 14" x 22" (35.6 x 55.9cm)
  11 rectangles, 14" x 18" (35.6 x 45.7cm)
  9 squares, 14" x 14" (35.6 x 35.6cm)
  2 rectangles, 14" x 10" (35.6 x 25.4cm)

Preparing the T-Shirts

T-Shirt

1 Cut your chosen T-shirts along the side seams, up the shoulders, and across the neck so there will be a finished rectangular shape around the motif of each T-shirt.

2 Sort the T-shirts into small, medium, large, and extra-large designs. With the painter's tape, label each shirt with size category and the corresponding block size you intend to cut.

    Small: 12½" x 8½" (31.8 x 21.6cm)

    Medium: 12½" x 12½" (31.8 x 31.8cm)

    Large: 12½" x 16½" (31.8 x 41.9cm)

    Extra-large: 12½" x 20½" (31.8 x 52.1cm)

3 Following the instructions for stabilizing T-shirts on page 22, back all your tees with the corresponding interfacing block and cut out. By previously labeling the T-shirts by size, you will know which interfacing block pairs with each shirt and which size block to cut.

Adapting for the Number of Shirts

If you want to include more than 23 shirts, combine some extra-small and small shirt motifs into a larger-size template (12" x 12" [30.5 x 30.5cm] or 12" x 16" [30.5 x 40.6cm]) to fit this pattern (see "Joining T-Shirt Logos" on page 24). Make sure you label these changes. If you have fewer than 23 shirts, fill in the gaps with fabric blocks of similar colors. Always remember to add seam allowances before you cut when joining pieces.

Building the Quilt

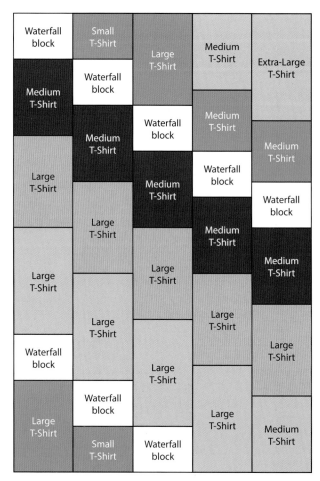

1 Arrange your prepared T-shirts and white Waterfall blocks into five columns according to the quilt layout diagram. When placing the blocks into the columns, make sure that the size of the T-shirt block matches the size in the layout diagram.

2 Label the back of each block. For the first column, start at the top and label the blocks A1, A2, A3, etc. For the second column, label B1, B2, B3, etc., until you have all five columns labeled.

3 Once you have labeled your columns, start at the bottom and place each block on top of the next. Make sure the "bottom block" is on the bottom. You will have five column stacks with block 1 of each column on top.

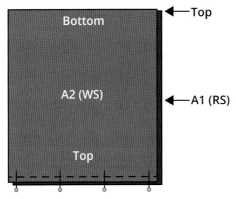

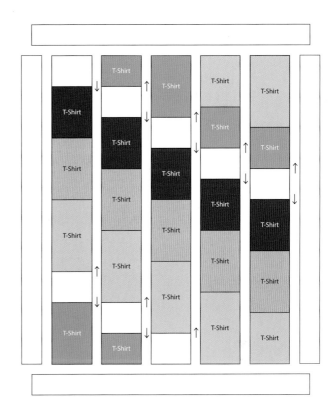

4 Beginning with column A, place block A2 (medium T-shirt block) upside down on block A1 (Waterfall block) right sides together. Make lower edges even and pin. Stitch across the lower edge with a ¼" (6mm) seam allowance. Open, and press the seam allowance away from the Waterfall block. Blocks A1 and A2 are now joined.

Note: In this design, the only block intersections that abut involve Waterfall blocks. If you always press away from the Waterfall block, your seams will nest when you join the columns together. When joining T-shirt to T-shirt, press the seam allowance toward the darker shirt.

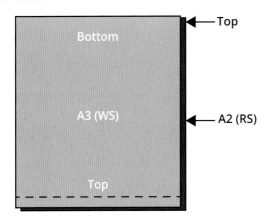

5 Repeat step 4 down the column, remembering to always place the next block upside down on the preceding block. As you are pinning and sewing the columns, check to make sure that the sewn blocks are the finished length you need them to be. If you cut accurately and are using an accurate ¼" (6mm) seam allowance, it should yield the correct result.

Note: Even stabilized knits can skew slightly at the corners. If this happens, use a rotary cutter and ruler to square up your blocks after stitching.

6 Once you finish sewing all five columns, sew column A and B together, then column AB to column C, then column ABC to column D, and finally column ABCD to column E. Make sure as you sew each column together that the intersections are aligned where indicated in the pattern (Waterfall blocks) and you square up any edges or corners on your cutting mat if needed. Press seam allowances open.

7 Join a 4" x 78" (10.2 x 198.1cm) border strip to each side of your quilt. Press the seam allowance toward the border. Trim any excess border at the top or bottom in line with the quilt top. Repeat with the remaining 2" x 70" (5.1 x 177.8cm) border strips, joining them to the top and bottom of your quilt.

8 Layer backing fabric, batting, and quilt top, and bind as desired.

Modern Oblique T-Shirt Quilt

By Sherilyn Mortensen

A unique and stunning quilt, this Modern Oblique design ups the T-shirt quilt game. The gray-and-white patchwork blocks create the illusion that it's all pieced on an angle, when in reality the blocks are traditionally pieced squares alternating with sashed T-shirts blocks and joined in rows. Very clever.

Finished Size: 80" x 96" (2 x 2.4m)
¼" (6mm) seam allowance (unless otherwise noted)

Materials

- 15 T-shirts blocks
  Unfinished block size: Fifteen 15" x 15" (38.1 x 38.1cm)
- ⅔ yard (61cm) each of different gray prints (I used 8 prints)
- ⅔ yard (61cm) each of different low-volume white prints (I used 8 prints)
- 5¼ yards (4.8m) backing fabric
- 6½ yards (5.9m) 100% cotton fusible interfacing
- 352" (8.9m) of binding (10 strips)

Cutting

From gray prints
  8 block squares, 9½" x 9½" (24.1 x 24.1cm)
  15 block squares, 5½" x 5½" (14 x 14cm)
  15 block rectangles, 4½" x 8½" (11.4 x 21.6cm)
  15 block strips, 4½" x 12½" (11.4 x 31.8cm)
  14 sashing strips, 1¼" x 16" (3.2 x 40.6cm)
  14 sashing strips, 1¼" x 17" (3.2 x 43.2cm)
From white prints
  8 block squares, 9½" x 9½" (24.1 x 24.1cm)
  15 block squares, 5½" x 5½" (14 x 14cm)
  15 block rectangles, 4½" x 8½" (11.4 x 21.6cm)
  15 block strips, 4½" x 12½" (11.4 x 31.8cm)
  16 sashing strips, 1¼" x 16" (3.2 x 40.6cm)
  16 sashing strips, 1¼" x 17" (3.2 x 43.2cm)

Making the Blocks

1 Prepare your T-shirts with interfacing as described on page 22. Cut 15 T-shirts blocks 15" (38.1cm) square, positioning your logos as desired.

2 Referring to "HSTs and Chain Stitching Blocks" on page 30, make the following:

Make 15

2a 15 gray/white 8½" (21.6cm) HST units, using 9½" (24.1cm) gray squares and 9½" (24.1cm) white squares. Press seams open.

Make 30

2b 30 gray/white 4½" (11.4cm) HST units, using 5½" (14cm) gray squares and 5½" (14cm) white squares. Press seams open

 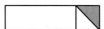

3 To make one gray/white pieced block, begin by sewing one gray/white 4½" (11.4cm) HST unit to the left side of one 4½" x 12½" (11.4 x 31.8cm) gray strip. Press seam allowance toward the strip. Sew one 4½" x 8½" (11.4 x 21.6cm) white rectangle to the left side of one 8½" (21.6cm) gray/white HST unit, then sew one 4½" x 8½" (11.4 x 21.6cm) gray rectangle to the right

side of same HST unit. Press seam allowances toward the rectangles. Sew one 4½" (11.4cm) gray/white HST unit to the right side of one 4½" x 12½" (11.4 x 31.8cm) white strip. Press the seam allowance toward the strip.

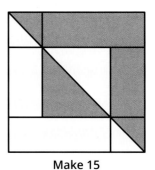

Make 15

4 Sew the three units from step 3 together to finish the block. Block measures 16½" (41.9cm). Make 15 blocks.

Building the Quilt

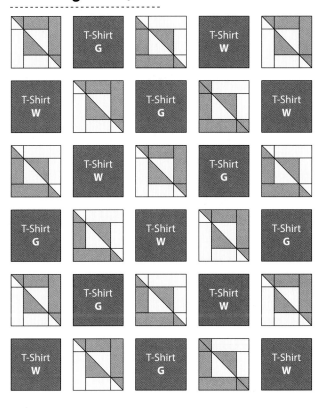

1 Arrange 15 T-shirt blocks and 15 gray/white 16½" (41.9cm) pieced blocks, alternating as shown. Pay attention to direction of gray/white pieced blocks. Decide placement of each T-shirt block.

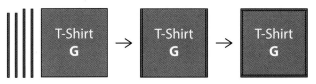

2 Sew two gray 1¼" x 16" (3.2 x 40.6cm) sashing strips to opposite sides of a T-shirt block marked *G*; refer to illustration. Trim sashing to fit and press seam allowance toward sashing. Then add two gray 1¼" x 17" (3.2 x 43.2cm) sashing strips to remaining sides. Trim to fit and press seam allowances toward sashing. Repeat for all T-shirt blocks marked *G*.

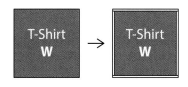

3 In like manner to step 2, add white sashing to T-shirt blocks marked *W*; refer to illustration.

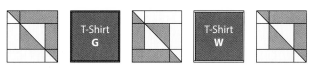

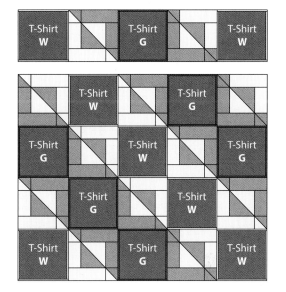

4 After gray and white narrow sashing has been added to the T-shirt blocks, sew blocks into rows of five and press. Join the rows and press. Take care to nest seams when possible.

5 Layer, quilt, and bind as desired.

Funfetti Caramel T-Shirt Quilt

By Olesya Lebedenko

My T-shirt quilt idea started at the caramel shop when my daughter and I were watching how the colorful caramel sweets were turned in an illuminated showcase. We came home and my daughter gave me the T-shirts she loved but grew out of. There were eight T-shirts, truly not too many. Most of them were very simple but truly treasured by her. Holding those T-shirts, I understood that the best way to mix them with design interest was to use Crazy Patch blocks, squares, and strips, which I pieced in sections first, then joined together to complete the quilt top.

Finished Size: 55" x 75" (1.4 x 1.9m)
¼" seam allowance throughout

Materials

- 5 T-shirts with logos
  Unfinished block size:
  Two 10½" x 10½" (26.7 x 26.7cm)
  One 13" x 13" (33 x 33cm)
  One 13½" x 12" (34.3 x 30.5cm)
  One 6½" x 6" (16.5 x 15.2cm)
- 3 T-shirts with all-over prints
  Unfinished block size:
  One 10½" x 10½" (26.7 x 26.7cm)
  One 8" x 8" (20.3 x 20.3cm)
  One 5½" x 5½" (14 x 14cm)
- 1 yard (91.4cm) total of assorted pink and red prints
- 1½ yards (1.4m) blue crackle print for sashing
- 2 yards (1.8m) solid-navy fabric for borders*
  *If you'd prefer to piece your border strips,
    1 yard (91.4cm) will suffice
- 2 yards (1.8m) 100% cotton fusible interfacing
- 1⅞ yards (1.7m) batting
- 3⅔ yards (3.4m) backing
- 270" (6.9m) of binding (7 strips)
- Optional: Masking tape

Cutting

Note: Numbers in brackets indicate the piece number (see quilt top diagram on page 112). Label each unit/block/piece as you cut or finish to avoid confusion later. Mark directly on the back of each piece with a wash-away marking pen or use masking tape labels. For example, #4 B, #15 E, #15 G, etc.

From pink and red prints
  12 strips total for strip blocks [#5, #10, #19, #22], 2½" (6.4cm) x WOF
  1 [#2] strip, 13" x 3" (33 x 7.6cm)
  1 [#16] strip, 25½" x 3" (64.8 x 7.6cm)

From blue print
  3 [#3] strips, 13" x 3" (33 x 7.6cm)
  6 [#4] strips, 8" x 3" (20.3 x 7.6cm)
  1 [#6] strip, 27" x 5½" (68.6 x 14cm)
  2 [#8] strips, 13" x 4" (33 x 10.2cm)
  2 [#9] strips, 17½" x 4¼" (44.5 x 10.8cm)
  2 [#11] strips, 8" x 4½" (20.3 x 11.4cm)
  2 [#13] strips, 22½" x 3" (57.2 x 7.6cm)
  4 [#15] strips, 25½" x 3" (64.8 x 7.6cm)
  6 [#17] strips, 5½" x 3" (14 x 7.6cm)
  2 [#18] strips, 44½" x 3" (113 x 7.6cm)

From navy
  2 border [#23] strips, 68½" x 5½" (174 x 14cm)
  2 border [#24] strips, 53½" x 5½" (135.9 x 14cm)

Preparing the T-Shirts

1 Select six of your T-shirts for single blocks. Prepare your T-shirts with interfacing as described on page 22:

Two unit G [#21] blocks: 10½" (26.7cm) square

One unit F [#21] block: 10½" (26.7cm) square

One unit F [#20] block: 5½" (14cm) square

One unit D [#14] block: 13" (33cm) square

One unit C [#7] block: 8" (20.3cm) square

Note: Do not discard the T-shirt backs; the extra T-shirt fabrics used for block #20 and block #21 are also used for smaller pieces in the Crazy Patch blocks.

2 The Crazy Patch blocks, #1 and #12, are made using templates. To ensure you have enough stabilized fabric for each piece, separate your remaining T-shirt fronts and backs and stabilize the entire front area. If you are using small children's T-shirts with an all-over print, stabilize the back as well. Stabilize the remaining T-shirt backs from step 1.

Making the Crazy Patch Blocks

1 Using the templates on page 113, trace each piece to the prepared T-shirt fabric and quilt cotton fabric of your choice and cut out. Label each piece with 1–9 for Block #1 and 1–6 for Block #12.

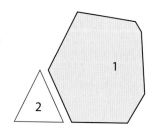

2 Starting with Block #1, place piece 2 on top of piece 1, right sides together, making sure to align the sides. Stitch with a scant ¼" (6mm) seam allowance. Press seams open.

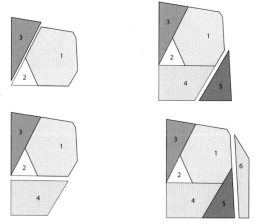

3 Repeat this procedure, stitching and pressing seams open. Add the pieces in order as shown.

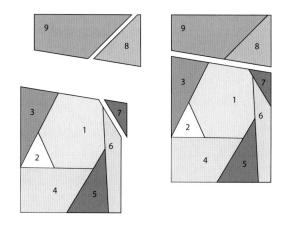

4 Once you've completed your Crazy Patch block, check that it measures 18" x 27" (45.7 x 68.6cm). Trim accordingly.

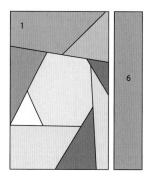
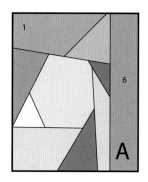

5 Join one strip [#6] to the right of the Crazy Patch block [#1] to complete unit A. Press seams toward blue print.

6 Repeat steps 1–4 for Block #12. Block should measure 15½" x 8" (39.4 x 20.3cm).

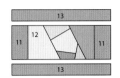 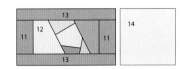

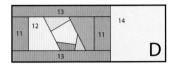

7 Join one strip [#11] to either short side of the Crazy Patch block [#12]. Then join one strip [#13] to the top and bottom of the block unit. Press all seams toward blue print. Join T-shirt block [#14] to the right of the Crazy Patch block [#12] to complete unit D. Press seams toward T-shirt block.

8 Label your two finished Crazy Patch blocks and set aside.

Making the Strip Blocks

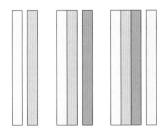 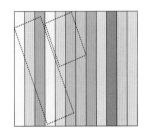

1 Join together the assorted 2½" (6.4cm) print strips into 12 rows. Press seams open.

2 Cut your strip set in half at the vertical center, then join the two sections together along the horizontal edge.

3 The strip sections in the quilt are cut on an angle. Using a straight edge and wash-away marking pen, draw the cutting guidelines for each rectangle at an angle and cut the following pieces from your strip block:

One unit G [#22] rectangle: 20½" x 5½" (52 x 14cm)

Two unit F [#19] rectangles: 15½" x 5½" (39.4 x 14cm)
One unit C [#10] rectangle: 18" x 5½" (45.7 x 14cm)
One unit E [#5] rectangle: 8" x 5½" (20.3 x 14cm)
One unit B [#5] rectangle: 8" x 5½" (20.3 x 14cm)

4 Label each piece.

Building the Quilt

Note: After joining each piece, press seam allowances toward blue or navy fabric.

1 Before beginning your assembly, group all the labeled pieces together by unit letter, A–G. Make sure you have all the pieces required for each unit.

 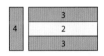

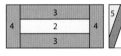 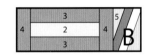

2 For unit B, first join strip [#2] between two [#3] strips. Add one strip [#4] to each short end. Then add strip block [#5] to the right to complete unit B.

    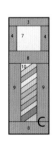

3 For unit C, join one strip [#9] to either long side of strip block [#10]. Join one strip [#8] to the top and bottom. Set aside this section. Join one strip [#4] to each side of T-shirt block [#7]. Join strip [#3] to the top to complete the second section. Join your second section to the top of your first to complete unit C.

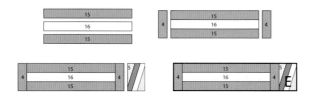

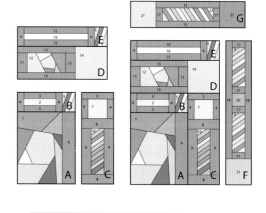

4 For unit E, join one strip [#15] to the top and bottom of strip [#16]. Join one strip [#14] to either short side. Then join strip block [#5] to the right to complete unit E.

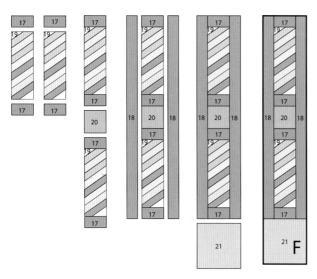

5 For unit F, join one strip [#17] to the short top and bottom of each strip block [#19]. Join one of these sections to the top and the other to the bottom of T-shirt block [#20]. Join one strip [#18] to each long side of the previous section. Join T-shirt block [#21] to the bottom to complete unit F.

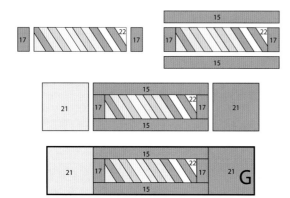

6 For unit G, join one strip [#17] to each short side of strip block [#22]. Add one strip [#15] to the top and bottom. Join one T-shirt block [#21] to each side to complete unit G.

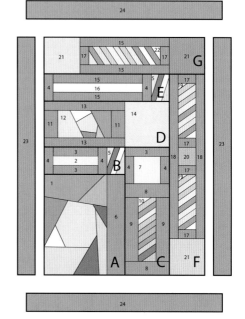

Quilt Top Diagram

7 Now that units A–G are complete, arrange them as shown. Join in the following order:

    Unit B to the top of A

    Unit C to the right of A/B

    Unit D to the top of A/B/C

    Unit E to the top of A/B/C/D

    Unit F to the right of A/B/C/D/E

    Unit G to the top of A/B/C/D/E/F

8 Join border strips [#23] to the quilt sides. Join border strips [#24] to the top and bottom and press to complete your quilt top.

9 Layer, quilt, and bind as desired.

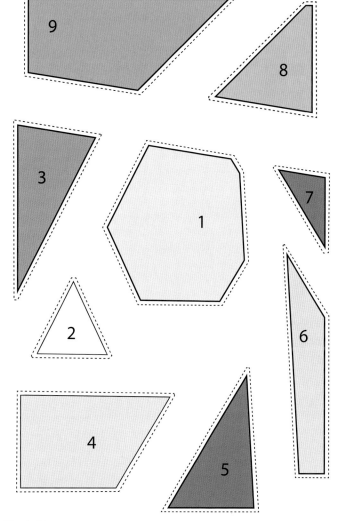

Block #1
Photocopy at 500%

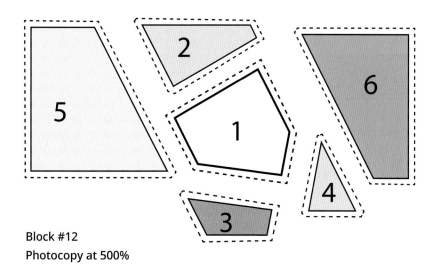

Block #12
Photocopy at 500%

Onesie T-Shirt Quilt

By Stephanie Soebbing

The Onesie T-Shirt Quilt is constructed of 9" (22.9cm) finished blocks, so in that respect, once you've created your blocks, finishing the quilt top is simply a matter of laying out your blocks and joining the rows together. Easy-peasy. Creating the blocks, however, is a bit of a "choose your own adventure" process. They're designed to use newborn to 2-year-old children's T-shirts, pants, and bibs as the center of a Log Cabin block. When finished, the smallest centers measure 3" (7.6cm) and are surrounded by Log Cabin strips; the largest are 9" (22.9cm), completely filled with a T-shirt and no Log Cabin strips.

No two quilts will end up the same because each one depends on how many articles of clothing you want to include and what size the block centers will be. For my quilt, I used 100 clothing items to make a queen-sized quilt—10 blocks across and 10 blocks down—using all seven possible size options for garment block centers.

Finished Size: 90" x 90" (2.3 x 2.3m)
¼" seam allowance throughout

Materials

Because this quilt is so variable, that means a standard yardage requirement chart can't be created. Instead, gather your baby and toddler clothes and cut the square centers. You can choose between 3½" (8.9cm), 4½" (11.4cm), 5½" (14cm), 6½" (16.5cm), 7½" (19.1cm), 8½" (21.6cm), and 9½" (24.1cm) squares for your 100 block centers.

Experienced quilters may enjoy adjusting the number blocks in their quilt. Refer to the Quilt Size Chart on page 120.

The charts that follow will help give you an idea of what the Log Cabin blocks of each size look like and the strips required for each size.

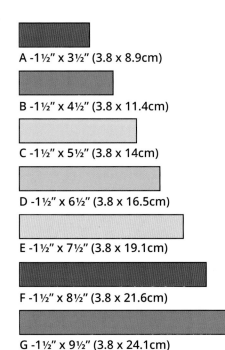

A -1½" x 3½" (3.8 x 8.9cm)

B -1½" x 4½" (3.8 x 11.4cm)

C -1½" x 5½" (3.8 x 14cm)

D -1½" x 6½" (3.8 x 16.5cm)

E -1½" x 7½" (3.8 x 19.1cm)

F -1½" x 8½" (3.8 x 21.6cm)

G -1½" x 9½" (3.8 x 24.1cm)

T-Shirt	T-Shirt	T-Shirt	T-Shirt	T-Shirt	T-Shirt	T-Shirt
A -0	A -0	A -0	A -0	A -0	A -0	A -1
B -0	B -0	B -0	B -0	B -0	B -1	B -2
C -0	C -0	C -0	C -0	C -1	C -2	C -2
D -0	D -0	D -0	D -1	D -2	D -2	D -2
E -0	E -0	E -1	E -2	E -2	E -2	E -2
F -0	F -1	F -2	F -2	F -2	F -2	F -2
G -0	G -1	G -1	G -1	G -1	G -1	G -1
9½" center	8½" center	7½" center	6½" center	5½" center	4½" center	3½" center

	A	B	C	D	E	F	G
3½" Center	1 x # = # of A strips	2 x # = # of B strips	2 x # = # of C strips	2 x # = # of D strips	2 x # = # of E strips	2 x # = # of F strips	1 x # = # of G strips
4½" Center		1 x # = # of B strips	2 x # = # of C strips	2 x # = # of D strips	2 x # = # of E strips	2 x # = # of F strips	1 x # = # of G strips
5½" Center			1 x # = # of C strips	2 x # = # of D strips	2 x # = # of E Strips	2 x # = # of F strips	1 x # = # of G strips
6½" Center				1 x # = # of D strips	2 x # = # of E strips	2 x # = # of F strips	1 x # = # of G strips
7½" Center					1 x # = # of E strips	2 x # = # of F strips	1 x # = # of G strips
8½" Center						1 x # = # of F strips	1 x # = # of G strips
Total Needed	Total # A strips	Total # B strips	Total # C strips	Total # D strips	Total # E strips	Total # F strips	Total # G strips
WOF Strips Needed	Cut # of 3½" x WOF strips	Cut # of 4½" x WOF strips	Cut # of 5½" x WOF strips	Cut # of 6½" x WOF strips	Cut # of 7½" x WOF strips	Cut # of 8½" x WOF strips	Cut # of 9½" x WOF strips

Use the formulas in the cell rows to determine how many of each size Log Cabin strip are needed for each block. Then add the columns to determine how many of each Log Cabin strip size are needed for the entire quilt.

There's a little bit more math to determine how much yardage you need. Keep in mind you're going to be cutting strips across your fabric yardage (WOF) that measure from top to bottom the length of the strip you need. Then, you crosscut 1½" (3.8cm) strips vertically across your WOF. By cutting across your WOF strip, no matter how long a strip you need, you will yield 28 strips that are each 1½" (3.8cm) wide and the same length.

I've included a handy chart below to help you figure out how many WOF strips you will need for different numbers of Log Cabin strips:

# OF LOG CABIN STRIPS NEEDED	# OF WOF STRIPS TO CUT
0–28 Log Cabin strips	Cut one WOF strip
29–56 Log Cabin strips	Cut two WOF strips
57–84 Log Cabin strips	Cut three WOF strips
85–112 Log Cabin strips	Cut four WOF strips
113–140 Log Cabin strips	Cut five WOF strips
141–168 Log Cabin strips	Cut six WOF strips
169–196 Log Cabin strips	Cut seven WOF strips
197–224 Log Cabin strips	Cut eight WOF strips
225–252 Log Cabin strips	Cut nine WOF strips

Once you know how many WOF strips you need for each size Log Cabin strip, you can add the total width together to come up with the total yardage needed. For example, for my quilt of 100 garments, I needed:

- One 3½" (8.9cm) x WOF strip = 3½" (8.9cm) total
- Two 4½" (11.4cm) x WOF strips = 9" (22.9cm) total
- Three 5½" (14cm) x WOF strips = 16½" (41.9cm) total
- Four 6½" (16.5cm) x WOF strips = 26" (66cm) total
- Six 7½" (19.1cm) x WOF strips = 45" (1.1m) total
- Seven 8½" (21.6cm) x WOF strips = 59½" (1.5m) total
- Four 9½" (24.1cm) x WOF strips = 38" (96.5cm) total

That all adds up to 197½" (5m) total needed or approximately 5½ yards of fabric.

For a scrappy look, I chose 12 different fabrics and opted to purchase ¾ yard or 27" (68.6cm) of each fabric. This would give me enough to make some cutting mistakes and have enough left for scrappy binding. This would mean 9 yards (8.2m) total, which is much more than the 5½ yards (5m) necessary; how much you decide to purchase all depends on your budget and how much experimenting you want to do. That's what makes this quilt unique!

I know that's a little more math than you are used to for a quilt pattern, but it is worth it to have an accurate amount of fabric and Log Cabin strips you need for your project.

Interfacing

Fusible interfacing is sold in 22" (55.9cm), 44" (1.1m), and even 60" (1.5m) widths, and the exact amount needed is going to depend on both the number and size of your T-shirt blocks. For the quilt shown, I purchased 4½ yards (4.1m) of 44" (1.1m) wide 100% cotton interfacing, which was more than adequate. Refer to "Stabilizing T-Shirts" on page 22 before cutting out any of your blocks.

Making the Blocks

1 Start by fusing the interfacing to the wrong side of the garments, making sure to match the size of the interfacing to the size of the garment.

2 Select a 3½" (8.9cm) garment block center, one A, two B, two C, two D, two E, two F, and one G Log Cabin strips. Arrange as shown below, with A directly above the block, and the sizes getting bigger in a clockwise direction.

3 Place the A strip right sides together with the top of the 3½" (8.9cm) garment block center. Sew together using a ¼" (6mm) seam and press the strip away from the garment block center.

4 Place one B strip right sides together with the right of the block center. Sew together and press the strip away from the block center.

5 Place one B strip right sides together with the bottom of the block center. Sew together and press the strip away from the block center.

6 Place one C strip right sides together with the left of the block center. Sew together and press the strip away from the block center.

7 Place one C strip right sides together with the top of the block. Sew together and press the seam open. You will press the seams open for the remainder of the block construction to help maintain an accurate finished block size.

8 Place one D strip right sides together with the right of the block. Sew together and press the seam open.

9 Place one D strip right sides together with the bottom of the block. Sew together and press the seam open.

10 Place one E strip right sides together with the left side of the block. Sew together and press the seam open.

11 Place one E strip right sides together with the top of the block. Sew together and press the seam open.

12 Place one F strip right sides together with the right side of the block. Sew together and press the seam open.

13 Place one F strip right sides together with the bottom of the block. Sew together and press the seam open.

14 Place the G strip right sides together with the left side of the block. Sew together and press the seam open. Block should measure 9½" (24.1cm) square.

15 Repeat steps 2–14 with remaining 3½" (8.9cm) garment block centers.

16 Select a 4½" (11.4cm) garment block center, one B, two C, two D, two E, two F, and one G Log Cabin strips. Arrange as shown on page 119, with B directly above the block center and the sizes getting bigger in a clockwise direction.

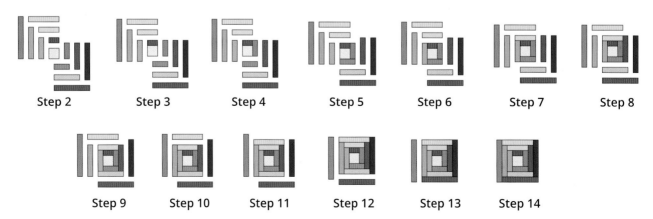

Step 2   Step 3   Step 4   Step 5   Step 6   Step 7   Step 8

Step 9   Step 10   Step 11   Step 12   Step 13   Step 14

17 Following the same method of construction for the blocks with 3½" (8.9cm) centers, begin sewing the strips to the block, starting with the B strip on top and working your way around clockwise. For all strips joining the garment block center, press the seams toward the strip; press the seams open for the remaining strips. Blocks should measure 9½" (24.1cm) square when finished. Repeat with remaining 4½" (11.4cm) garment block centers.

18 Select a 5½" (14cm) garment block center, one C, two D, two E, two F, and one G Log Cabin strips. Arrange as shown, with C directly above the block center and the sizes getting bigger in a clockwise direction.

19 Following the same method of construction for the blocks with 3½" (8.9cm) centers, begin sewing the strips to the block, starting with the C strip on top and working your way around clockwise. For all strips joining the garment block center, press the seams toward the strip; press the seams open for the remaining strips. Blocks should measure 9½" (24.1cm) square when finished. Repeat with remaining 5½" (14cm) garment block centers.

20 Select a 6½" (16.5cm) garment block center, one D, two E, two F, and one G Log Cabin strips. Arrange as shown, with D directly above the block and the sizes getting bigger in a clockwise direction.

21 Following the same method of construction for the blocks with 3½" (8.9cm) centers, begin sewing the strips to the block, starting with the D strip on top and working your way around clockwise. For all strips joining the garment block center, press the seams toward the strip; press the seams open for the remaining strips. Blocks should measure 9½" (24.1cm) square when finished. Repeat with remaining 6½" (16.5cm) garment block centers.

22 Select a 7½" (19.1cm) garment block center, one E, two F, and one G Log Cabin strips. Arrange as shown, with E directly above the block and the sizes getting bigger in a clockwise direction.

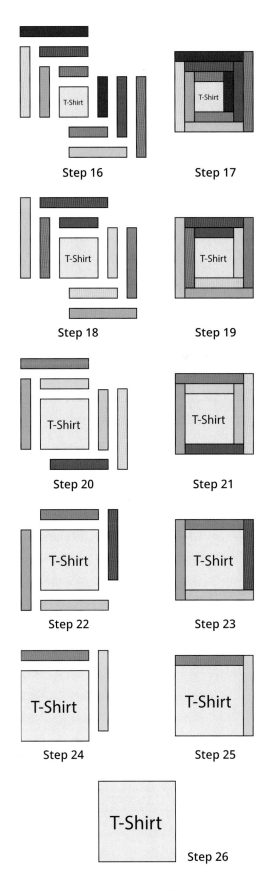

Step 16   Step 17

Step 18   Step 19

Step 20   Step 21

Step 22   Step 23

Step 24   Step 25

Step 26

23 Following the same method of construction for the blocks with 3½" (8.9cm) centers, begin sewing the strips to the block starting with the E strip on top, working your way around clockwise. Press the seams toward the strip for all strips. Blocks should measure 9½" (24.1cm) square when finished. Repeat with remaining 7½" (19.1cm) garment block centers.

24 Select an 8½" (21.6cm) garment block center, one F, and one G Log Cabin strips. Arrange as shown on page 119, with F directly above the block and G on the right.

25 Sew the F strip on top and the G strip to the right side of the block. Press the seams toward the strip for all strips. Blocks should measure 9½" (24.1cm) square when finished. Repeat with remaining 8½" (21.6cm) garment block centers.

26 No sewing is needed for the 9½" (24.1cm) garment block centers. They will be included in the quilt as is with no strips sewn to the sides.

Quilt Size Chart

If you don't have 100 garments for this quilt or have a specific project in mind, the Onesie T-Shirt Quilt is easy to adjust. This handy chart shows you how to adapt this project to your needs:

QUILT SIZE	FINISHED SIZE	# OF BLOCKS	# OF BINDING STRIPS	BACKING
Crib	36" x 45" (91.4 x 114.3cm)	20	Five 170" (4.3m)	1½" yards (1.4m)
Lap	63" x 63" (1.6 x 1.6m)	49	Seven 262" (6.7m)	4 yards (3.7m)
Twin	63" x 90" (1.6 x 2.3m)	70	Eight 316" (8m)	5⅔" yards (5.2m)
Queen	90" x 90" (2.3 x 2.3m)	100	Ten 370" (9.4m)	8⅓" yards (7.6m)

Building the Quilt

1 Arrange the garment blocks in a design that is pleasing to you.

2 Sew the blocks into horizontal rows. Press the seams open when they are made of quilting cotton. Press away from the garment when the join includes a 9½" (24.1cm) garment block center.

3 Join the rows to complete the quilt top.

4 Layer, quilt, and bind as desired.

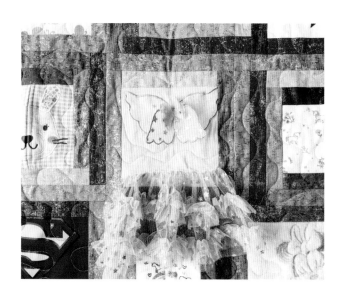

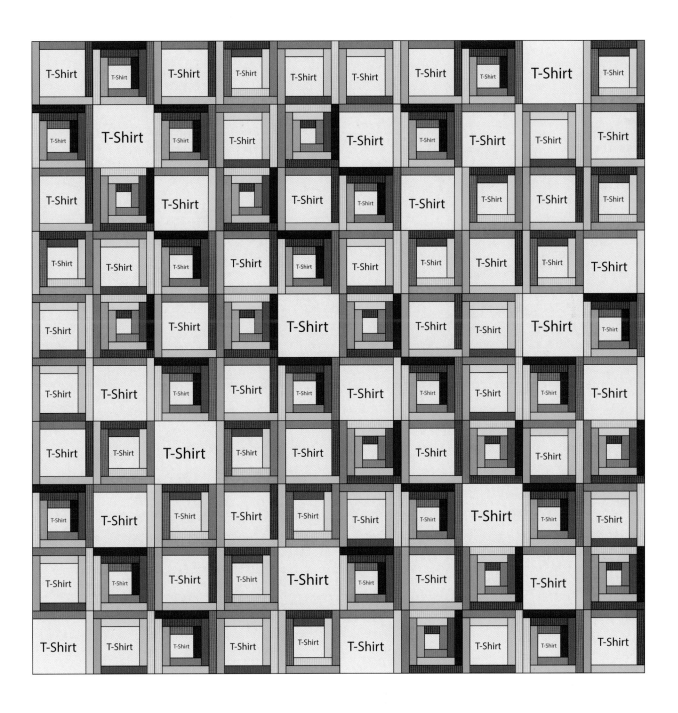

Glossary

Basting: Temporary stitching to hold layers of fabric together; meant for easy removal. Can be done by hand or machine, or with pins or fabric glue.

Block: Completed pattern of pieced fabric. Blocks are arranged together to a make a quilt pattern.

Binding: Strip or strips of fabric that covers the raw edge of a quilt to finish it. Generally, ¼" (6mm) or ½" (1.3cm) wide.

Chain piecing: Technique of sewing units together without cutting the thread holding them together. The thread is then cut at the end to create individual pieces.

Free motion quilting: Technique to create an easy range of motion when sewing into layers of fabric. Achieved by lowering the feed dogs and hovering over the surface. This allows decorative patterns to be sewn into the layers.

Fussy cutting: Selecting a specific section, often a flower or a character, to emphasize or frame it in your finished project.

Hanging sleeve: Tube or series of loops attached to the back of a quilt to prepare the finished product for display. A rod or dowel is inserted, like a curtain.

HST: Half-Square Triangle. A square unit made by joining two triangles.

Interfacing: Thin piece of fabric attached to the wrong side of fabric to reinforce and prevent stretching. Can be sewn or adhered with heat.

Long arm quilting: Technique similar to free motion quilting, but uses an industrial longarm machine instead of a home sewing machine. Quilts the layers of a quilt together. Long arm services are available at quilting and sewing machine shops for a fee.

Machine quilting: Stitching through layers of fabric with a sewing machine.

Miter: A diagonal fold or seam at a corner.

Nesting seams: Pressing nearby seam allowances to the right and left (opposite of one another) to better allow the fabric to lay flat.

Patchwork: See piecing.

Piecing: Sewing together small cloth shapes to create a pattern.

Piping: Narrow trim stitched around a piece for reinforcement and decorative purposes.

Pivot: Technique for machine stitching around angular corners. Stop the machine with the needle down, raise the presser foot, turn the fabric, lower the presser foot, and continue stitching.

Precuts: Fabrics cut to specific sizes and by fabric manufacturers, often in bundles of coordinating colors or prints.

Quilt back: Traditionally a whole piece of cloth or two joined pieces. Can also be pieced fabric. The back should be made or cut larger than the quilt top, 5"–6" (12.7–15.2cm) all around, because the quilting process may gather the fabric and reduce the overall size.

Quilting: Process of sewing together a quilt sandwich.

Quilt sandwich: A quilt top, batting, and quilt back fabric. These three layers are required to finish any quilt.

Quilt top: A created length of fabric for the face of a quilt. Often consisting of blocks, rows, columns, and borders.

Right side: The front of the fabric; most noticeable when there is a pattern.

Rough-cut: Cutting around an element, leaving space on all sides.

Sashing: Pieces of fabric that separate blocks or rows of blocks.

Seam allowance: Usually ¼" (6mm) of fabric that extends beyond where pieces of fabric have been joined.

Selvage: The finished edges on woven fabric. Generally cut off and discarded before using fabric for a project.

Squaring up: Using a clear square ruler, tracing paper, or straight rulers to evenly trim a larger block or unit to size.

Stay stitch: Stitches meant to hold layers or reinforce curved edges. Can prevent stretching or be used for stability.

Stitch-in-the-ditch: A technique for quilting by sewing directly in the join of a seam.

Strip piecing: Sewing together long pieces of fabric into a set, then cutting to the needed block size.

Topstitch: A line of machine stitching on the front of a garment.

Whipstitch: Joining one piece of fabric to another by sewing one edge with small stitches over the edge.

WOF: Width of fabric.

Wrong side: The back of the fabric; most noticeable when there is a pattern on the opposite side.

Index

A

air-erase pens, 12
art markers, 13

B

backing, 34
bag project
    cross-body, 42
    tote, 76
basting, 122
batting, 14
Bento Box block, 86
Big Flight T-Shirt Quilt, 90
binding, 36, 122
    calculating, 36
    joining ends, 38
    machine edge stitch finish, 39
    quilt edges, 38
    whipstitch finish, 38
block, 122
    Bento Box, 86
    Bright Hopes, 54
    Crazy Patch, 108
    Flying Geese, 92
    Log Cabin, 114
    star, 60, 66
    strip-pieced, 84, 111
block layouts, tip, 41
Bright Hopes block, 54

C

chain piecing, 31, 122
chain stitching blocks, HSTs and, 31
clear ruler, 10
Concert Tee Wall Hanging, 52
Crazy Patch blocks, 110
crib quilt size, 120
Cross-Body College Bag, 42
cutting mat, 12
cutting T-shirts, 20

D

dorm pillow, 48
duckbill scissors, 12
duplicate block, fixing with color, 64

F

fabric glue stick, 15
fabric markers, 13
fabric shears, 12
fabric, 16
    fussy cutting, 33
    precuts, 16
    quilt backing, 34
    yardage, calculating for Log Cabin
      block quilt, 114
Flying Geese block, 92
free motion quilting, 122
Funfetti Caramel T-Shirt Quilt, 108
fusible web, 15, 117, 122
    alternative to, 96
fussy cutting, 33, 122

G

glossary, 122

H

half-square triangles. *See* HSTs
hanging sleeve, 122
    making a, 58, 122
hanging tabs, making, 68, 122
HSTs, 30, 62, 72, 106, 122
    and chain stitching blocks, 30
    pressing tip, 62
    squaring up, 32

I

Improv Column T-Shirt Quilt, 94
interfacing, 15, 117, 122
    alternative to, 96
iron, 9
    pressing T-shirts, 20
    tip, 13

J

joining T-shirt logos, 24

K

Kid's Character T-Shirt Quilt, 60
Kid's Character Wall Hanging, 66

L

lap quilt size, 120
learning to quilt, 30
Log Cabin block, 114, 118
    calculating yardage for, 114
logos
    cutting from T-shirt, 20
    extending with fabric, 29
    joining, 24
    pressing, 13, 20
    stabilizing, 22
long arm quilting, 36, 122

M

machine edge stitch finish, binding with,
    39
machine feet, 9
machine quilting, 122
markers, fabric and art, 13
marking pens, 12
    air-erase, 12
    wash-away, 12
miter, 122. *See also* binding
Modern Oblique T-Shirt Quilt, 104

N

needles, 9
nesting seams, 30, 122
No Waste Flying Geese method, 90

O

Onesie T-Shirt Quilt, 114

P

painter's tape, tip, 11
Pellon FF78F1 Flex-Foam 1-Sided Fusible web, 15
Pellon SF101 Shape-Flex, 15
pillow
    project, 48, tip for, 14
pillow forms, 14
pinking shears, 12
pins, 10
    curved, 10
piping, 122
    tip for applying, 52
pocket, for water bottle, 76
Precut Dorm Pillow, 48
precuts, 16, 122
    pillow using, 48
pressing, tip for seams, 62
pressing cloth, 13
pressing T-shirts, 20

Q

queen quilt size, 120
quilt back, 34, 122
    incorporating T-shirts on, 35
quilt batting, 14
quilt, binding edges of, 38
quilting, 122
    binding, 36
    design inspiration, 18
    long arm, 36
    tools and notions, 8
quilt project, 60, 70, 84, 90, 94, 100, 104, 108, 114
quilt rulers, 10
    clear, 10
    square, 10
    triangle, 10
quilt sandwich, 35, 122
quilt size chart, 120

R

Rectangle-Block T-Shirt Quilt, 70
rotary cutters, 12
ruler
    clear, 10
    quilting, 10
    seam guide, 14
    square, 10
    Stripology, 11
    triangle, 10

S

sashing, 122
scissors, 12
    duckbill, 12
    fabric, 12
    pinking, 12
    sewing, 12
seam allowances, 9, 21, 122
seam guide ruler, 14
seam, nesting, 30, 122
selvage color dots, 16
sewing machine, 8
    feet, 9
    needles, 9
sewing scissors, 12
Sharpies, 13
square ruler, 10
stabilizing T-shirts, 22
    alternative to, 96
star block, 60, 66
stay stitch, 122
steam iron, 9
    pressing T-shirts, 20
    tip, 13
stitch in the ditch, 122
strip block, 84, 111
strip sets, for piecing, 96
Stripology ruler, 11
Sulky Stick 'n Stitch, 15

T

template paper, printable, 15
template quilting, 33
template star pattern, 64
topstitch, 122
tote project, 76
tracing paper, 11
triangle ruler, 10
T-Shirt Tote for a Cause, 76
T-shirts
    cutting, 20
    incorporating on quilt backs, 35
    joining logos, 24
    pressing, 20
    prewashing, 19
    stabilizing, 22
    working with, 19
twin quilt size, 120
Two-Block T-Shirt Quilt, 84

W

wall hanging project, 54, 66
wash-away marking pens, 12
water bottle pocket, 76
Waterfall T-Shirt Quilt, 100
wax paper, 11
whipstitch finish, binding with, 38, 122
WOF, 122

Y

yardage, calculating for Log Cabin block quilt, 114

Z

zipper top for tote, 7

Photo Credits

Step-by-step photography and all other photography (unless otherwise stated) by Amelia Johanson

Studio photography by Mike Mihalo: front cover (all), 1, 3, 4–5 (all), 7, 18, 33, 39, 40–41 (all), 43, 49, 55, 59 (right), 61, 67, 77 (all), 83 (bottom right), 85, 91, 95, 101, 105, 106 (bottom right), 109, 125, back cover (projects)

Additional photography by Chase Johanson: 35 (top), 71, 73 (bottom), 74 (bottom)

Additional photography by Stephanie Soebbing: 115, 120

Additional photography by David Fisk: 80 (bottom right)

All illustrations (unless otherwise stated) by Mary Ann Kahn

Illustrations by Kristin La Flamme: 92–93 (all)

Illustrations by Olesya Lebedenko: 110–113 (all)

Illustrations by Stephanie Soebbing: 114, 116, 118–119 (all), 121

Christmas Confetti quilt © Lynette Jensen, photos by Craig Anderson and Dennis Kennedy: 18 (left)

Shutterstock photos: leungchopan (model: 2, back cover), Pixel-Shot (6), PopTika (backgrounds: 55, 61, 67, 71, 85, 91, 95, 101, 105, 109, 115), Olga Miltsova (54–55 guitar), PhotoProAD (76), Sanit Fuangnakhon (85 football),

About the Author

Amelia Johanson has been sewing for herself and others for thirty years. Previously an editor of *Sew Beautiful* magazine and a current contributor to *Classic Sewing* magazine, she has also written for several other sewing publications. Additionally, Amelia has tech edited, contributed to, and co-authored a number of sewing and quilting books and is also a Martha Pullen Licensed Instructor. With degrees in journalism and home economics from the University of Missouri, she has spent her career combining a passion for both the written word and clothing design. She and her incredibly supportive husband, Michael, have raised three particularly tall boys who have been the recipients of many an altered or custom garment through the years. She authored Laudauer's *Pocket Guide to Fasteners* in 2021.

About the Contributors

Jane Haworth is a British-born quilt artist and teacher living in Auburn, California. She has been sewing and crafting all her life. Jane attended art school in Carlisle, England, to study textile design, and her first real job was making clothes on the production line for Laura Ashley in North Wales. This job provided professional training on an industrial sewing machine and experience in a factory setting, which provided great roots for a quilting career.

Jane only became aware of quilting after her family relocated to California from the UK in 1998. She now loves to share her quilting and fabric collage passion with students all over the globe. She teaches students from quilt guilds, shops, and shows, even traveling to Dubai in February 2020 to teach a workshop on collaging faces. Jane is also a returning teacher at IQF Houston, Road to California, and Craft Napa. Her work has been exhibited at many major quilt shows and won numerous awards. Her published articles have appeared in *Quilting Arts* magazine, she has appeared on Quilting Arts TV, and she is releasing her first book with Landauer in fall 2023.

Kristin La Flamme is currently the Fabric Coordinator at Montavilla Sewing Centers in Portland, Oregon. Among other tasks, she creates shop-hop projects, works on complimentary patterns, and shares her expertise on combining color and pattern with an eager clientele. Her BFA is in graphic design, and she worked in Los Angeles and Washington, DC, before embarking on life as an army wife. Those years, with their frequent moves, offered opportunities that inform her artwork with personal insights and social commentary. She's shown her art quilts internationally in group and solo shows and is a coauthor of *Twelve by Twelve: The International Art Quilt Challenge* published by Lark Crafts. She's working on her first book with Landauer, which will be a perfect complement to *Patchwork T-Shirt Quilts*.

Olesya Lebedenko is an artist from Ukraine living in Canada, where she works and creates modern template designs. She is a teacher, designer, quilter, doll maker, author, magazine contributor, and entrepreneur as the founder and owner of Olesya Lebedenko Design. Her work has been featured in American, Canadian, and Ukrainian publications; she has written countless tutorials and articles, and she has led hundreds of workshops all over Europe and Canada. Olesya is a professional member of the International Quilt Association and the Canadian Quilters' Association. In 2020, she became a BERNINA Canada Ambassador. To learn more about Olesya Lebedenko and to view her work, visit her website (www.olesya-l-design.com), her Instagram(@olesyalebedenkodesign), and her Etsy shop (www.etsy.com/shop/OlesyaLebedenkoDsgn).

Olesya has written several books with Landauer focusing on quilting and gift sewing, including *Sewing Scrap Blocks with Character*, *Sewing Cozy Craft Projects*, and *Adorable Appliqué Sewing Projects*.

Sherilyn Mortensen is the proud owner of Sea Sherilyn Sew. She is a pattern designer, teacher, presenter, and long arm custom quilter. She is a quilt artist for Gammill and thoroughly enjoys her association with them. As a self-taught quilter, Sherilyn has improved and fine-tuned her skills throughout the years. Her passion for quilting began about 25 years ago. After gathering up some old clothes and scraps of fabric, she cut up a bunch of squares and pieced together a large, king-sized quilt. Although it was not perfect, she loved it and knew her love affair with quilting had begun. To this day she still enjoys the entire quilt-making process, from the first steps of designing to the last steps of quilting. Whether quilting with others, for others, or for herself, quilting will always be one of Sherilyn's greatest joys and pleasures in life, and it has definitely been one of the best forms of therapy! Her love and passion for quilting is equally shared with her joy of being a wife, mom, gramma, daughter, sister, friend, and author. Her first book, *Quilting Through the Year*, was published with Landauer in 2021.

Jill Nelson is the designer behind Jilly Bean Sewing. She has been sewing for over 32 years, during which her skills have evolved from sewing bags and clothing, teaching kids to sew, pattern critiquing for youcanmakethis.com (Kimberbell Designs), selling made-toorder items on Etsy, and now creating custom T-shirt/memory quilts. She is also learning long arm quilting at AQPS Raliegh Thread Waggle Quilting. Jill has been married for 20+ years and has five children, including twins with special needs. She is an organizational guru, family oriented, sport-watcher/player, church/school volunteer, and outgoing person. Making custom items for her clients is one of her favorite things because they create new memories while preserving their family history for years to come. Her designs can be found at https://linktr.ee/jillybeansewing.

Growing up, **Stephanie Soebbing** had one goal: to make a career out of writing. Really, she just wanted to be creative, but it took some time to figure that out. She started her career as a journalist and then moved into digital marketing. While she was pregnant with her first child, Stephanie was looking for a way out of the rat race of the advertising world so she could have more flexibility to be with her daughter. That "way out" came when she started teaching students her first Block of the Month design at her local quilt shop. She published her pattern online and combined her marketing, storytelling, and video production training from her journalism days into her blog, QuiltAddictsAnonymous.com. It became a fast-growing pattern design company and online fabric store. Seven years later, those first students have turned into thousands of quilters worldwide who have been inspired by Stephanie's designs and video tutorials. Today she works with her husband at their online quilt shop in Rock Island, Illinois.

You can find more of Stephanie's original patterns at shop QuiltAddictsAnonymous.com and browse hundreds of free quilting tutorials at QuiltAddictsAnonymous.com/tutorials. Her books for Landauer include *Fat Quarter Patchwork Quilts*, *Simple Quilts for the Modern Home*, and *Fat Quarter Workshop*.